The Bread Ovens
of Quebec

To Paul and Rachelle Carpentier

Managing editor: Viviane Appleton
Text editor: Frances Smith
Production supervisor: Donald Matheson

Design by Jacques Charette and Associates Ltd.
Text set photocomposition in Souvenir type face by M.O.M. Printing
Colour separations by Bomac Batten Ltd.
Book printed on Renaissance stock by M.O.M. Printing

The Bread Ovens of Quebec

Lise Boily
Jean-François Blanchette

National Museum of Man
National Museums of Canada

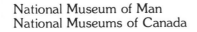

©National Museums of Canada 1979

Canadian Centre for Folk Culture Studies
National Museum of Man
National Museums of Canada
Ottawa, Canada K1A 0M8

Catalogue No. NM92-48/1979

Printed in Canada

ISBN 0-660-00120-9

Édition française
Les fours à pain au Québec
ISBN 0-660-00004-0

Contents

Acknowledgements

We wish to thank those whose valuable support enabled us to carry out this work. Mr. Jean-Paul Simard of the Université du Québec à Chicoutimi encouraged us to undertake the fieldwork, and, in addition, persuaded his brother Louis-Joseph to build the oven that we describe in Chapter II. Dr. Carmen Roy, formerly Chief of the Canadian Centre for Folk Culture Studies at the National Museum of Man and now the Museum's Senior Scientist, Folk Culture, made it possible for us to develop and complete this study, which was of special interest to her. Mrs. Johanne Blanchette-Émond assisted us with the interviews during the summer of 1972; some of the sketches she made are reproduced in this book. To Paul Carpentier, who from our first meeting believed in the importance and value of the subject, we dedicate this work in appreciation of his dynamic approach in the supervision of our project.

We also wish to thank Dr. Robert Bergeron, Dean of Advanced Studies and Research, and Dr. Jean-Noël Jacob, Director of Audiovisual Services, both of the Université du Québec à Chicoutimi; the technical assistance they made available to us greatly facilitated our task of gathering information in the field and frequently helped us out in difficult situations. Our professors at the Department of Anthropology at Brown University in Providence, Rhode Island, were of great help, especially Professor James Deetz, who closely followed our progress and gave us much-appreciated encouragement.

We are grateful to all our kind informants and to the many researchers who share our interest and who, on occasion, guided us in our approach: Drs. Robert-Lionel Séguin, Thomas Lavoie and Luc Lacourcière; Messrs. Jean-Claude Dupont, Paul-Louis Martin, Fernand Caron, Marcel Moussette and Jean-Charles Magnan; and Mrs. Sylvie Vincent.

A special thank you also to the directors and staff of several research centres and archival collections: the Centre de documentation en civilisation traditionnelle of the Université du Québec à Trois-Rivières, the Centre de documentation de la Place Royale in Quebec City, the Laboratoire d'anthropologie amérindienne du Québec, the Archives de Folklore de l'université Laval, the Bibliothèque nationale du Québec, and the Société historique du Saguenay.

For the original French-language edition of this work, we owe a great debt to the interest of Norman Boudreau, former Chief of Publications, and to Madeleine Choquette-Delvaux, editor; we offer them our sincere thanks for their constructive criticism in the editing of the French manuscript. We also wish to thank Frances Smith and Viviane Appleton for their editing of the English translation.

Introduction

"The bread oven is not merely a bread oven."
This may seem a strange opening remark for a work entitled *The Bread Ovens of Quebec,* but we wish to stress that these ovens are used not only for baking bread, but for other culinary and domestic purposes as well. Furthermore, as a material product of a particular culture, the bread oven is also related to the economic, social, linguistic, psychological, religious, and other cultural subsystems.*

Our study seeks to demonstrate the usefulness of combining research on the material culture with other elements making up the cultural whole. Far from being simply an object, the bread oven reflects a technique, a physical environment, a standard of living, a spatial organization, indeed a whole a way of life. It reveals a great deal about the perceptual and conceptual schemes of the people using it. The oven may therefore be considered a total cultural fact.

The study of the bread oven also relates to the increasingly widespread concept of "foodways". "This concept of foodways refers to the whole interrelated system of food conceptualization and evaluation, procurement, distribution, preservation, preparation, consumption, and nutrition shared by all the members of a particular society."[1] Our treatment of the bread oven as part of the overall culture naturally includes this concept.

A rigorous system of research enabled us to gather considerable documentation from various archival collections and numerous informants, especially in rural Quebec. The most informative people were from the Saguenay-Lac-Saint-Jean region, Charlevoix, Montmorency, Beauce, Lotbinière, and the south shore of the St. Lawrence River as far as the tip of the Gaspé Peninsula.

Our research was conducted in three main phases: a study of the literature, research of archival documents, and fieldwork.

The first phase uncovered only a very small amount of information. There is, in fact, very little material on bread ovens in studies that have appeared thus far. There are, however, some general works on French-Canadian folk culture that deal with the subject briefly. We will mention just a few of these.

Among the most recent studies, we should mention those of Robert-Lionel Séguin, who notes the presence of the oven in the

---

*The reader may wish to consult the works of James Deetz, Lewis Binford, and David Clarke, which discuss the link between the cultural subsystems and the importance of considering material culture within its overall context.

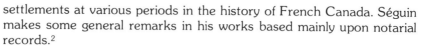

settlements at various periods in the history of French Canada. Séguin makes some general remarks in his works based mainly upon notarial records.[2]

On a lighter note, Félix-Antoine Savard includes in one of his works a charming description of Alexis, a tireless builder of clay ovens. In a delightful allegory, the author gives us a detailed and highly informative description of the phases of construction.[3]

We should also mention the very useful writings of Georges Bouchard, a professor at the School of Agriculture in Sainte-Anne-de-la-Pocatière at the beginning of the twentieth century. He offers those interested in agronomy, and the layman as well, some very valuable advice on the small-scale production of clay ovens.[4]

Our curiosity even led us to consult French literature on the subject, in an attempt to compare the methods used by French-Canadian *habitants* with those used by the peasants of France. In so doing, we were fortunate to come across the very first encyclopaedia by Diderot and d'Alembert.[5] This scientific work, which seeks to understand and depict an object as it truly is and to show its origin, tells of a procedure for constructing a bread oven at very little cost.[6] The method described is still used today by some Quebec farmers.

Finally, we should point out that we eliminated all possibility of the existence of seigneurial ovens by consulting authors who clearly state that this seigneurial right was never exercised in New France.[7] This is not to say, however, that the seigneurs did not have their own ovens to meet the needs of the manor.

The second stage of our research involved the examination of some notarial records of the French Regime.[8] In studying these documents we noted that bread ovens were mentioned only occasionally.[9] When they are referred to, the date shown is for the day they were spotted and does not always indicate the date of construction. Consequently, an oven could well have existed for a hundred years but only appear in the records for the first time when it was already obsolete. Moreover, the records do not necessarily include all those who used the ovens. The contracts reveal that, in the city, workmen—often masons—were sometimes hired to construct or rebuild a bread oven. This was not the case in the country, however, where the assistance of a neighbour or other local inhabitant with the necessary skill could be obtained. In such circumstances, the services rendered would be compensated for in food or lodging, and a visit to the notary would thus not be necessary. Nor would there be any written record when an individual built his own oven. If rural people were capable of putting up their buildings themselves or with the help of nearby neighbours, they certainly would have been able to make their own ovens as well.

In view of the above, the archives do not tell the whole story of the ovens, and, consequently, the facts we gleaned from them should be interpreted carefully.

The third and not the least important phase consisted of careful fieldwork. We cannot overemphasize the importance of the valuable information given to us by our two hundred informants, which enabled us to reach certain general conclusions valid for all the regions visited. Furthermore, our fieldwork enabled us to consider the bread oven within the overall context of rural life. During our visits, we were able to see a full range of oven sites and to assess the significance of the location of the ovens in relation to household activities as a whole. Our work in the field also gave us a better understanding of the construction techniques used, and enabled those interviewed to express themselves freely and naturally in their own colourful way.

Our informants were questioned in a very objective manner. We asked only neutral questions, in an attempt to respect the scientific methodology of ethnography. According to the precepts of ethnography, it is important for the researcher to stay in the background in any interview with an informant. The informant can then express freely, in his own words, what he knows and has experienced. The interviewer is always careful to avoid any leading questions that might alter the original thought of the informant. Throughout our investigation, we judged an interview a success if our informant was appalled at our ignorance and decided to set us straight right away. It was in this way that people's perceptions of the bread oven were transmitted to us, and they did this in the terms peculiar to rural Quebec.

In the first chapter, we analyse the information collected on the ovens and the people who built them. In the second chapter, we present a technical study of the building of a clay oven in the Saguenay region to familiarize the reader with the construction of ovens of this type. You will note that the technique used is the same as the one described by Diderot in his *Encyclopédie,* which was first published between 1751 and 1765. We then move on to the chapter on bread making, where we present the information required for a proper evaluation of this source of nutrition. And, finally, we cover the oral tradition relating to the bread oven and everything connected with it.

On the whole, the picture of the bread oven that we present is basically a historical reconstruction and does not depict the situation that exists in rural Quebec today. We do feel that it is valid for the turn of the century, however, since the average age of our informants was seventy.

Baking day—a nostalgic picture of rural
life
Notman Collection,
Public Archives of Canada,
no. C-20615

Outdoor clay oven
Saint-François concession, Saint-Urbain
(Charlevoix county)
Blanchette Collection, CCFCS Archives, no. 113*

*CCFCS: Canadian Centre for Folk
Culture Studies, National Museum of
Man, Ottawa

Semi-indoor oven forming part of a
detached building
Concession 5, Saint-Hilarion (Charlevoix
county)
Blanchette Collection, CCFCS Archives, no. 104

Chapter I

The Ovens

We should first make a distinction between brick, clay, and stone ovens; the type is determined by the material used for making the dome. The material varies not according to the period, but rather to the wealth of the people and to the availability of suitable raw materials in the surrounding area. In our fieldwork we learned that people usually preferred to use some inexpensive material that was within easy reach.* To build an oven at very little cost, what better material could be found than clay or stone? Village brickyards often provided an inexpensive product, such as bricks from less successful firings. If people had more money, they bought better-quality bricks and often went so far as to import them.

Secondly, we noticed a difference in the sites of ovens: some were outdoors and others indoors, and we believe it is extremely important to define clearly each of these two categories.

The outdoor ovens are completely separate from the house or are set apart in the yard and protected by a simple shelter. In each region studied we noticed that, though the oven was located not far from the dwelling, it was positioned so that the prevailing winds would not blow smoke or sparks towards the house.[1]

Indoor ovens can be found on the ground floor, in the cellar, in a lean-to, or in a detached building, and may be either wholly or partly indoors.[2] They are all connected to a chimney.

We believe that distinguishing between indoor and outdoor ovens reflects domestic realities. Ovens equipped with a chimney serve specific household needs; in providing the room with necessary ventilation, the chimney makes it possible to carry out other tasks. It thus links the oven with the household's indoor life.

In previous studies on rural dwellings in French Canada, the indoor life of the household had always been considered as limited to the inside of the house; everything outside the house was related to outdoor life. We believe that this interpretation does not reflect reality as expressed (either explicitly or implicitly) by our informants. According to our informants, the separate building in which the oven was often located should be considered as a second component of the dwelling, which the whole family occupied and worked in during certain periods of the year. From early spring until late fall a variety of household chores were performed there, such as bread making, washing, cleaning and dressing

---

*We should point out that, in work camps, cooking was often done on portable steel ovens or over burning embers.

flax, carding, smoking meat, drying vegetables, rolling tobacco, and even preparing and sharing meals.

It appears that during certain times of the year, depending on socio-economic circumstances not yet studied sufficiently, household tasks and leisure activities took place in different buildings. For practical considerations as well as psychological well-being, family routines were patterned in accordance with the weather and the seasons. This change of surroundings, adding as it does a new dimension to the rural way of life, deserves further study and interpretation.

Outdoor Ovens

In this section we will be discussing clay, brick, and stone ovens. **Clay ovens** are made by a mudwalling technique and are built in the shape of a horseshoe.[3] These thick-walled ovens make the best bread. Simply constructed, they have a base, insulating material, a hearth, framework, doors, a dome, and a shelter. A description of each of these parts will help us to better appreciate these inexpensive ovens, which were very popular at a time when the need for self-sufficiency on the farm compelled people to use natural materials.

Levelled earth or the flat side of a rock is most often used as a natural foundation for the base, which may be made of wood, stone, or cement. Among the types of wood commonly used, cedar is preferred because it resists rot and is long-lasting.[4] Next in popularity are pine, ash, balsam fir, cypress, tamarack, or black spruce. Four cedar logs used as legs are stood on end on the ground or on large flat stones and are held in place by small joists on the top. A deck made of spruce or ash logs is laid on these joists. Sometimes thick boards are braced to form a cage instead of erecting vertical posts. The platform can also take the form of a footing made of fieldstones held together by clay or mortar. This masonry is laid about one foot (30 cm) down in the ground.[5] As a buffer, sand is inserted between the stones, which are used because they are so readily available and are more fire-resistant than other materials.

Sometimes an insulating material is used between the frame and the hearth. We noted this addition in the description of a number of ovens. A large flat stone formed a base for the hearth and the doors,[6] but these days cast iron[7] or sheet metal[8] are being used instead. It is also possible to apply directly on the deck a layer of clay reinforced with straw,[9] a row of bricks,[10] or stones held together with clay.[11] Some people even use cedar bark or jute as insulation and to prevent the clay from slipping through the spaces in the flooring.[12]

The hearth, or platform, on which the bread dough is laid to cook is generally made of one thickness of blue clay from steep riverbeds or riverbanks that have rich and heavy soil. The choice of the material is important, since it influences the efficiency of the cooking and the durability of the oven. The ideal clay breaks like soap,[13] is granular, blue,[14] crumbly, sticky,[15] and "tough". In the Malbaie region, the clay[16] would be taken from the Clermont[17] slopes. On Île aux Coudres, along the banks of

Brick oven
Concession 8, Saint-Honoré (Dubuc county)
Blanchette Collection, CCFCS Archives, no. 54

Clay oven
Saint-Simon-de-Rimouski
Blanchette Collection, CCFCS Archives, no. 201

Oven with brick dome covered with fieldstones
Kamouraska
Blanchette Collection, CCFCS Archives, no. 194

Clay oven with ornamentation on the clay collar, or ridge
Saint-Laurent concession, Baie-Saint-Paul
Blanchette Collection, CCFCS Archives, no. 106

Brick and mortar oven
Saint-Antoine concession, Baie-Saint-Paul
Blanchette Collection, CCFCS Archives, no. 120

Clay oven
Saint-François concession, Saint-Urbain
Blanchette Collection, CCFCS Archives, no. 113

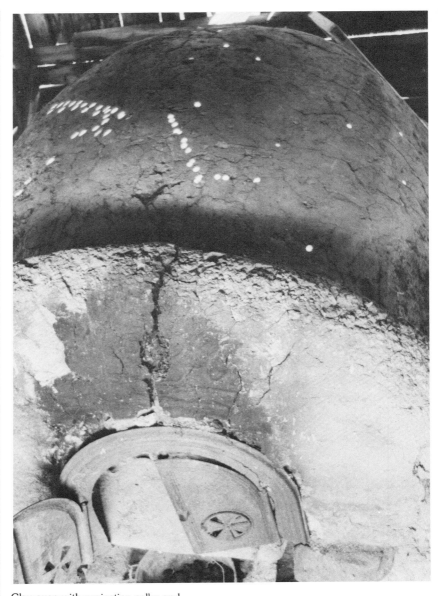

Clay oven with projecting collar and
well-shaped dome
Saint-Louis concession, Saint-Fulgence
(Dubuc county)
Lise and Jean-François Blanchette Collection

the Saguenay River, as well as at Petite-Rivière and in the Lower St. Lawrence region, such clay can be found along the foreshores at low tide.[18] In Beauce, near Scott, the clay can be found near the brickyards.[19] At Sainte-Anne-de-Chicoutimi it can be taken from the Terres Rompues.[20]

The clay is pounded, worked, or trodden upon in a simple trough, or a horse can be used to tread it under its hooves.[21] Straw is generally added as a binding material, but millet, a type of dry hay called *taigne*,[22] salt hay,[23] horse hair,[24] or cow hair[25] are also used; other additives are sand to dry, thin,[26] and reduce the stickiness of the clay, or perhaps salt to harden it[27] and make the mixture waterproof. Salt is used in the Gaspé Peninsula, in particular. Once the worked soil breaks apart easily in chunks, it is used to build up a generous coat on the surface of the base or on the insulating material, wherever necessary. A good eight inches (20 cm) of this mixture is uniformly applied and allowed to harden naturally. The thicker the covering, the better the oven heat is retained.[28] In some regions, the circumference of the hearth is marked with a belt of quarry stones, which help to retain the clay and support the dome.[29]

We noted a certain diversity in the materials used for the hearth. Sometimes flat fieldstones are held together by a mortar made of quicklime, sand and water, or by clay.[30] Sometimes the hearth is made of bricks, set either on edge or flat, in loose sand or clay. The joints are filled with mortar, clay, sand, or cement.[31] Sometimes there is a double row of bricks.

Once the hearth is completed, the doors (generally made of cast iron) are put on. These doors play an important role in the design and the roughcast of the dome. They are put in place on the front of the hearth even before the framework is erected. The most common models are semicircular in shape[32] and may be described as follows. A shelf 10 inches (25.4 cm) wide forms the threshold of the oven. A frame decorated with simple mouldings and soldered to this shelf forms an arch-shaped opening; the hinges that support the double doors are attached to the front of the opening, one on each side. The doors are held closed by a depression in the threshold. Each of the double doors is decorated with a stylized sheaf design and has small air holes cut out at the bottom. The arch-shaped opening to which the doors are attached slopes inward to form a slightly oblique ledge 5 inches (12.7 cm) wide; this ledge not only supports the flexible branches used for the framework, but also makes it easier to shape the protective ridge, or collar. The doors are 23 inches (58.4 cm) wide and 18 inches (45.7 cm) high on the outside. They are cast in sand moulds, and their place of origin is frequently shown on the frame above the two doors. The inscription, when used, appears like this: BERNIER LOTBINIÈRE or BERNIER. Some doors do not bear any inscription.

This model was not the only one that existed. At the Méthot foundries in Lotbinière another type was made, in the shape of a semipolygon. It is very decorative, the frame made in fine, fluted lines, with leaf-work all around it. Four hinges are used to hold two iron bars

Sometimes a large flat rock is used as a
base for the doors
Saint-Augustin, lac Saint-Jean
*Blanchette Collection, NMC (National
Museums of Canada) 73-25922*

Oven built on a base of logs
Saint-Honoré (Dubuc county)
*Blanchette Collection,
NMC 73-25915*

Door resting on a row of bricks
Fortierville (Lotbinière county)
Blanchette Collection,
NMC 73-26005

The baker's peel and the fire rake are
the most used oven tools
Blanchette Collection,
NMC 73-25979

An old oven door made of wood and
held in place by a long pole
Anse Saint-Jean (Saguenay county)
Blanchette Collection,
NMC 73-25973

Style of door called *oeil de bouc* ("goat's
eye")
Blanchette Collection, CCFCS Archives

Semipolygonal door
Blanchette Collection, CCFCS Archives

supporting the doors, which are decorated with floral designs and have small air holes at the bottom. The door sill is crescent-shaped. The inscription MÉTHOT, when used, runs along the base. The manufacture of these rare crescent-shaped doors was stopped before that of arched doors.[33]

These two main models of iron doors date from the second half of the nineteenth century, and seem to follow the development of the foundries mentioned:

The Bernier and Méthot foundries in Lotbinière poured double doors for bread ovens. These are the only two documented examples that I know of, and foundries probably manufactured such doors after 1852.[34]*

It should also be noted that some people mentioned as the manufacturers of their doors the Terreau-Racine foundry in Quebec City or small local foundries, such as the one run by Euchariste Lavoie in Baie-Saint-Paul, among others. It is difficult to determine exactly when oven doors were first manufactured in Quebec. Nevertheless, the information we obtained shows that under the French Regime iron doors did not exist,[35] and that it is possible that the ones we know are the result of a series of adaptations.

Then, and sometimes even now, other types of doors were used to close the ovens. They were constructed very crudely and often consisted of a single wooden door, which was wrapped with wet cloth during the baking. Old metal hoops resting on a flat rock, hewn stones arranged to form a square opening, or old bricks arched or piled side by side were used to make a frame. During the baking, the opening was closed by a wooden door covered with sheet metal and held in place by a wooden beam or perhaps an enormous flat rock.[36] Square, rectangular or semicircular single or double doors of old furnaces were also used, as well as pieces of sheet metal propped up by long poles. In 1918, Georges Bouchard gave the following interesting description:

The opening of the oven was most often framed by an old bottomless cauldron and old discarded metal wheel-rims from carts. Later on, doors from cast-iron stoves were used. A cauldron lid, a piece of bare wood, or wood covered with sheet metal was used to close the opening.[37]

In this way, even before using foundry products, the *habitant*, or farmer, used his imagination to find appropriate solutions to his everyday problems.

Once the hearth is firmly set on its base, the framework, or form, for the dome is erected. Among the materials used for this framework are young trees, barrels, wet sand heaped in the shape of a dome, layers of turf, and metal cart-wheel rims. This list requires further explanation.

The most common form of framework consists of a lattice of alder branches.[38] If alder is not available, hazel, aspen, or young birch are substituted, depending on which is most abundant. After the wood is

---

*Unless taken from English texts, quoted passages throughout have been translated from the original French.

worked to make it more pliable, a basic form is constructed; preferably this will be higher at the back, in accordance with the oldest and best technique,[39] to ensure good hot-air circulation in the oven. The ends of the branches of supple wood are stuck through the edge of the hearth until they touch the deck, or the top part of the footing. The framework is first constructed lengthwise (from the rear to the ledge above the doors), and then shorter, older branches are positioned across the width at regular intervals. At this stage the resulting lattice already reveals the final shape of the dome. The bent branches are then attached together at intersecting points, using binding cord, twine, or fishing line.[40] Sometimes this latticework is strengthened by adding cedar bark,[41] gunny sacks,[42] or straw to hold the clay together and to avoid any unevenness on the inside of the dome.

Small barrels that formerly held flour, apples, or molasses were occasionally used as a model for the form.[43] A barrel was laid on the hearth, fixed in position, and several pieces of wood were attached to the sides and covered with strips of turf to complete the required shape.[44]

Occasionally, wet well-compacted sand was used.[45] The sand was used alone, or firewood was piled up "to the right height and then sand was placed on it, higher at the back than at the front".[46] Compressed clay could also be used for the form,[47] as was done by an old craftsman at Cap-au-Corbeau. There were other variations, such as the use of old sleigh-runner fittings covered with chicken wire,[48] or wooden cages rounded out with dried hay.[49]

In spite of all these possibilities, we should stress that alder frames appear to be the most suitable, since clay domes contract slightly, due to the evaporation of water, as they dry out in the air. If the frame is made of flexible wood, it will easily withstand shrinkage and thus avoid the cracking that sometimes occurs with metal frames.[50]

The clay used for the dome is chosen according to the same criteria as those for the hearth. A blue clay, which is handled the same way as pottery clay and is combined with a filler, such as vegetable or mineral binding material, has the best texture. Blocks of clay combined with hay or sand are applied first to the sides and to the ledge over the doors, and then along the base of the frame. Lumps weighing between 15 and 25 pounds (6.8 and 11.3 kg) are shaped and used to cover the framework. They are laid with alternating joints[51] and are levelled off and smoothed out by hand. Special attention is given to the thickness of the walls, which should be between six and eight inches (15.2 and 20.3 cm) at the base. The top part of the dome is thinned for the sake of balance, but it is thickened at the front edge to form the ridge. This more-or-less pronounced ridge forms a collar around the doors. It acts as a barrier to the flame when the oven is lit,[52] and reinforces the structure around the door.[53] In certain regions, as in Charlevoix and Saguenay–Lac-Saint-Jean, the ridges sometimes have a clay ornament, such as a small figurehead,[54] or special conical finishing touches,[55] and sometimes they bear the date of construction.[56] The last stage is the smoothing of the dome: all the joints are filled in[57] and the surface is either worked by hand or tapped with a mallet. The rear part is

A metal hoop can be used for the door
frame
Saint-Gabriel concession, Sainte-Marie
(Beauce county)
Blanchette Collection,
NMC 73-25996

Framework of young branches for the
dome
Marius Barbeau Collection 1936,
NMC 81097

evened out, and the oven becomes smooth and shiny with the addition of a fine clay glaze as a sealer.[58] Sometimes the dome is protected with a layer of chalk or mortar.[59]

Then there is a wait of several days to allow the clay to dry and harden slowly before lighting the first fire. The drying period lasts at least eight to fifteen days.[60] The best results are obtained by allowing the oven to dry naturally, since sudden drying would cause it to crack. The oven is fired progressively by means of repeated small fires until the wood framework breaks apart and the clay becomes brick-red on the inside.[61] The oven is fired in the same way as a potter fires his pottery. Little by little, the dome contracts slightly and hairline cracks appear here and there. This is no cause for alarm: "As the cracks appear they are filled in with clay."[62] Diderot, in the eighteenth century, emphasized the special precautions to be taken during the drying process:

> We notice that the best ovens are those wholly constructed of clay and then allowed to harden gradually, in stages, until a very hot fire vitrifies the clay. In these ovens the bread bakes easily, perfectly, and for little cost, especially when the dome is not too high, when care has been taken to make the sides of the dome sufficiently thick, and when the cracks have been adequately repaired.[63]

Because of the possibility of damage in bad weather, the clay oven is protected by a wooden or sheet-metal shelter. This may be made of cedar, waste timber, or sheet-metal shingles curved over the dome, with the sides made of overlapping vertical boards.[64] The shape used varied: triangular, semicircular, or inverted U-shaped; sometimes the shelter had a slanted roof. In the Gaspé we noticed that shelters were not always used. A number of ovens were left exposed to the weather.[65] As we have already mentioned, the addition of salt to the clay makes the oven weatherproof to some extent. In order to protect the ground from the fire, a small terrace made of flat stones or old bricks would often be laid in front of the oven.[66]

In conclusion, clay ovens cost almost nothing and are quickly built—it takes only one full day, once the base is constructed. They are also very durable.

Exterior **brick ovens** are regular in shape and have simple lines. The oblong shape of the brick does not give the craftsman much scope for using his imagination. These ovens are more costly to build, requiring an exceptionally solid base made of stone, cement, or heavy wood, and a particularly resistant type of framework for the dome.

The platform is erected in the same way as for clay ovens. The hearth is made of brick rows, the bricks lying on edge or flat, and held together by mortar made of quicklime, sand, and water, or by ordinary cement. Occasionally fieldstones are used and covered with mortar,[67] or sometimes the bricks are coated with clay.[68] Something stronger than alder branches is needed for the framework: wooden arches can be cut to make an appropriately large dome; the dome can be constructed of two-by-fours;[69] a framework can be made of halved metal hoops;[70] or clay can be built up to the desired size and shape.[71] The bricks follow the line of the

Shelter known as the oven shed
Saint-Pierre concession, Bagotville
(Dubuc county)
Blanchette Collection,
NMC 74-14539

Clay oven with an ornamented
projecting collar, or ridge
Saint-Laurent concession, Baie-Saint-
Paul
Blanchette Collection, CCFCS Ar-
chives, no. 106

Clay oven found in Charlevoix. On the
collar of the oven are the remains of a
clay figurine made and put there for the
amusement of the children
Sainte-Mathilde
Blanchette Collection, CCFCS Ar-
chives, no. 86

domed support and are positioned flat, one on top of the other. At the bottom of the oven they are aligned on both sides, but as they reach the top of the dome they are set wider apart, as in the shape of a fan. The edge of the bricks gives the inside a uniform curve. Small pebbles and mortar are slipped between the bricks to preserve the shape of the arch and to fill in the joints.[72]

> Because the mould is curved, the sides of the bricks on the inside of the oven are almost touching, while on the outside they have larger spaces between them; these spaces will be filled with mortar mixed with small pieces of brick.[73]

The dome is coated with one thickness of mortar, clay, cement, or whitewash to preserve the brick and keep in the heat.[74] For greater protection, a wall of stones and mortar up to one foot (30 cm) thick is sometimes built against the sides of the dome.[75] In some areas, the oven is enclosed by a structure of large stones, and a clear idea of the appearance and actual size of the dome can only be obtained by looking inside the opening of the door and examining the inside of the oven.[76] A brick wall is often erected to form a façade. The doors, as well as the shelters, are similar to those used for clay ovens. Some brick ovens have an air hole either at the rear or at the top of the dome. This characteristic of both clay and brick ovens is rarely found in the Charlevoix region, but is common on the south shore of the St. Lawrence River and in the Lower St. Lawrence. The durability of these ovens depends upon the quality of the wet mortar used for the joints.

We were unable to find much information on **stone ovens**. Our fieldwork led us to old brick and clay ovens, and we found it most unusual that we did not find any specimens of stone ovens. Stone ovens date back many years, as there are references to them in the notarial records of the French Regime. In 1667, the notary Bénigne Basset described the estate of the late Jean Cicot and noted the presence of a stone oven: "A large chimney wall with its substructure also in masonry, and a decrepit stone oven. . . ."[77] On 27 March 1677, a contract "was made between the parties to the effect that the said lessor would make on the said leased concession, during the said lease, and construct, a chimney of masonry with a well-built stone oven."[78] Records of the notary Anthoine Adhémar, dated 5 February and 11 April 1699, contain two other references to limestone ovens.[79]

These records confirm the existence of stone ovens, but do not explain why they disappeared when others constructed so long ago managed to survive the passage of time. Were they very good for baking? How long did they last? How important were they? Our informants had very little to say on the subject. Furthermore, it is all too easy to mistake a brick or clay oven protected by a stone structure for one that has a skilfully constructed dome of quarry stones!

An oven with a brick dome, its sides and front protected by rough masonry
Kamouraska region
Blanchette Collection, CCFCS Archives, no. 194

A brick wall often forms the façade of brick ovens
Chambord (Roberval county)
Blanchette Collection,
NMC 73-25949

Oven with a brick dome, whose sides are protected by a wall of mortared fieldstones
Kamouraska
Blanchette Collection,
NMC 74-14626

The "Old Grey House" and its semi-indoor oven. The smaller house and the oven were built about 1850 and the large house in 1870.
Photograph of a pastel drawing by Mr. Philippe Gagnon, Chicoutimi, May 1972

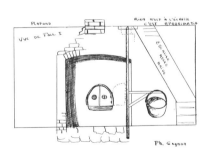

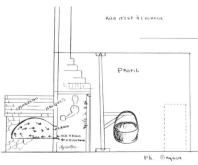

Front of the semi-indoor oven in the "Old Grey House"
Freehand sketch by Mr. Philippe Gagnon, Chicoutimi, May 1972
Blanchette Collection, CCFCS Archives, no. 32A

Cross-section of the same oven; its doors are set in the backplate of the fireplace
Freehand sketch by Mr. Philippe Gagnon, Chicoutimi, May 1972
Blanchette Collection, CCFCS Archives, no. 32B

Indoor Ovens

In our travels throughout the various regions of Quebec, we observed some very old ovens that are still standing, largely because of their location. In the cellar or on the main floor, partly or wholly indoors, and surrounded by stonework, these ovens are all connected to large fireplace chimneys, and their doors always open on to the main living area of the house or building in which they are located. There, baker and bread are protected from the weather.

The dates on catalogued models start from the middle of the eighteenth century and continue until the beginning of the twentieth.[80] The various parts and materials differ very little from those of the outdoor ovens described above. Nevertheless, we noted a regularity in the base, which is almost always a footing of large stones held together with mortar. Occasionally the base is constructed of squared timbers. The hearth is made of flat stones,[81] bricks,[82] or simply compressed clay.[83] The dome is basically an assembly of bricks or, very rarely, a symmetrical layering of clay blocks.[84] The ridge over the opening merges with the wall of the chimney, and the doors are set into the backplate or sides of the fireplace. The dome will thus be located behind the fireplace[85] or on either side of it.[86] In both cases it is necessary to reach the oven through the fireplace. There are some exceptions, such as ovens that are connected to the chimney by a pipe. The oven is then situated right beside the fireplace and has a separate opening, thus providing easier access to it.[87] Although in former times chimneys were often made of mud, those which have survived were made of fieldstones held together with mortar.

The Various Uses of the Oven

Bread ovens were, of course, used chiefly for baking bread, and we describe the technique in detail in a later chapter. But it is incorrect to assume that the bread oven was used solely to produce batches of loaves. Depending on seasonal requirements, it was used for a multitude of purposes. We obtained an enormous amount of information concerning these ovens, and the subject continues to arouse our curiosity. If only the ovens themselves could talk—they would have countless stories to tell!

After a baking session, it takes the oven at least twenty-four hours to cool down.[88] In former times, this lower temperature was used for different types of cooking. One of the favourite dishes was the pot of pork and beans, which was placed at the back of the oven, where the beans simmered slowly, filling the air with their almond-like aroma. During the holiday season, the oven was used for cooking *tourtières,** pot pies, ground-meat pies, and other meats, as well as dessert pies, cookies, buns,

---

*The term *tourtière* is commonly used to describe the well-known French-Canadian meat pie. Traditionally, in the Saguenay–Lac-Saint-Jean region, however, a *tourtière* is actually more like a deep-dish layered meat-and-potato pie.

Indoor Ovens

A detached building with oven
Blanchette Collection, CCFCS Archives, no. 104 (exterior)

Although its dome is outdoors, the oven can be opened from inside the building by doors in the backplate of the fireplace
Saint-Hilarion (Charlevoix county)
Blanchette Collection, CCFCS Archives, no. 104 (interior)

Semi-indoor oven in a building adjoining the house
La Baleine, Île aux Coudres
Blanchette Collection, CCFCS Archives, no. 141

Oven in a detached building
Saint-Gabriel concession, Baie-Saint-Paul
Blanchette Collection, CCFCS Archives, no. 142

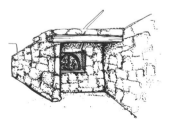

Semi-indoor oven in a detached building
Sainte-Hélène, Kamouraska
Blanchette Collection, CCFCS Archives, no. 196

Oven located in the cellar
Saint-Laurent, Île d'Orléans
Blanchette Collection, CCFCS Archives, no. 148

Semi-indoor oven forming part of a
detached building
Saint-Hilarion (Charlevoix county)
Blanchette Collection,
NMC 73-25993

Small detached building housing an oven
Saint-Gabriel concession, Baie-Saint-Paul
Blanchette Collection,
NMC 73-26061

Semi-indoor oven on the ground floor
Chicoutimi-Nord
Blanchette Collection,
NMC 74-14548

Semi-indoor oven forming part of a
building adjoining the house
Saint-Jean-Port-Joli
Blanchette Collection
NMC 74-14616

raisin cakes, and a large variety of fruit cobblers, such as the blueberry cobbler made in the Saguenay region during the summer months.[89]

As well as for cooking, the still-warm oven, with all its burning embers removed, was used as a sterilizer to disinfect the chicken, duck and goose feathers used for stuffing mattresses, pillows, or cushions. The feathers were first washed and stuffed into cotton or gunny sacks, and then dried in the oven for five or six days. The odours and parasites frequently found in the quills were killed by the heat.[90] During periods of illness, it was also a common practice to disinfect the clothing of the sick, as well as their dishes and straw mattresses.[91] This odd combination of culinary and medical functions bears eloquent witness to the transforming power of heat generated by an oven. The oven serves as a mediator for the necessary transformations.

At harvest time, the task of drying the flax was made easier by placing it in the oven prior to hackling it.[92] Bundles of flax were laid out on small iron bars to prevent them from becoming scorched on the hearth.[93] The bark protecting the fibre dried out and was thus easier to remove. "I can tell you that when we had flax to hackle for making thread and cloth, as soon as the bread was out we put the flax in the oven and that made it ready to hackle."[94] In *La Corvée*, published in 1917, the author refers to that particular use of the oven: "The old folks did not want to hackle hundreds of bundles of flax without help when drying them in the bread ovens."[95]

The oven was also used as a substitute for a drying room for fulling homespun cloth. Strips of wet cloth were rolled up and placed in the warm oven. The fulling was accomplished by the heat, and the weave gradually tightened up.[96] The oven was also used for drying herbs, such as parsley and savory, which were then used throughout the winter.[97] Carpenters also took advantage of the warm oven to dry out their wood; this practice is still common at L'Anse-Saint-Jean in the Saguenay.[98]

In the absence of a smokehouse, many *habitants* attached supports or iron hooks above the oven doors. They placed damp sawdust on the hearth, lighted it, and left the doors ajar. Burning slowly, the fire gave off smoke, which cured meat previously coated with molasses (giving it colour) and sprinkled with aromatic herbs. Sometimes the meat was left to soak in brine for a couple of weeks before smoking.[99]

Other, more ordinary tasks were also done in the oven after the baking was finished. Some women, for example, browned flour for stews,[100] while others stacked wood in the oven for the next baking.[101]

Tables

The two tables that follow sum up our archival research and our fieldwork. Table 1 shows the sporadic mention of ovens during the period under study, that is, from 1650 to 1740. A number of factors influenced the components of this table, since, as we mentioned at the beginning of this study, the notarial records give incomplete information with regard to the occurrence of these ovens. It is therefore difficult to draw conclusions.

Table 1
Occurrence of Ovens in Notarial Records, 1650 to 1740

	Indoor ovens					Outdoor ovens
	Buildings		Main floor	Cellar	Chimney not listed	
	Detached	Adjoining				

Clay oven

Brick oven

Stone oven

Material unknown

33

The dates cited in the table correspond to the year the oven was noted and not the year in which it was constructed.[102]

However, this table does show all the various types of ovens that existed at the beginning of the eighteenth century. We found a reference to an outdoor clay oven in a farming lease dated 1704, between Pre LeClerc and Jacques Gervais, with the following details: ". . . and an oven on this land made of clay, simply erected, separate from the house, and exposed to the air".[103] In 1709 an outdoor brick oven was noted: "A brick oven fitted with an iron ring at its opening and situated in the yard of the said house. . . ."[104]

We also find indoor ovens housed in detached buildings. In 1673, a reference was made to such ovens: "A little square building made of wood stacked one piece above the other, 17 feet long and 16 feet wide, with its floor made of planks of hewn timber. The chimney, constructed of masonry from the ground to the beam, with its foundation and the rest of the said chimney of mud-walling, and an adjoining clay oven at ground level. Its door closes with a bolt, and brass hooks and hinges, but no lock or key."[105] In May 1692, an agreement was reached between Louis Prat, on behalf of Louis Jolliet, and André Coutron to build a bakehouse, "and also to repair the oven, to reduce it, and to cover it with boards to protect it from water damage . . . and to finish building the chimney for the oven and raise it to the necessary height. . . ."[106] Later, in 1699, this same type of oven was reported in a rental lease: ". . . to have the lessor build an oven for baking bread with a capacity of about two and one-half minots next autumn and then to build a small building to be used as a bakery, closed and covered, next spring at the latest, after the next seeding. . . ."[107] The minot was an old French measure for grain;[108] it indicated the quantity of flour needed for one batch of bread and was thus used as a reference for the dimensions of the oven.[109]

Ovens situated in buildings adjoining the house appeared in several places. A sales contract for a house and property, dated 14 August 1700, specifies "a two-storey stone lean-to with oven and chimney that the said seller has constructed".[110]

Ovens on the main floor of a dwelling are also recorded, and one description dated 1698 is found in a lease that states that "the lessee agrees to have the ruins of the clay chimney belonging to the said house destroyed, and to build a new one of stone and clay on the same spot, together with a clay oven".[111]

Finally, various notarial documents list ovens located in the cellar. In a document dated January 1727, we have the details of an agreement between a certain Mr. Lapalme and Vincent Rorant in which we note the requirement to construct an oven in a cellar: ". . . to make and supply all the materials necessary for the construction of a thirty-foot-square building as agreed. . . . An oven in the cellar with a small chimney connected to the large chimney. . . ."[112]

When all the inventories from the French Regime have been examined we will be able to determine the chronological trends and possibly the geographical variants.

Our fieldwork led us to examine 113 ovens; and our informants were able to establish accurately the date of construction for 99 of them. The location of the ovens, and the effect this had on their durability, was the prime factor influencing our data. Very old ovens have survived because they were built indoors. Since there are a limited number of these, we have very little information on their occurrence. Some of those examined were constructed in the first quarter of the twentieth century (Table 2).

More exposed to the weather than the indoor ovens, outdoor ovens[113] survived for a shorter period of time. On the other hand, we found enough of them to be able to be more explicit about their importance from 1920 on. Table 2 shows an increase in the number of these ovens between 1920 and 1935. This increase corresponds to the beginning of a period of self-sufficiency that reached its high point around 1930. This phenomenon is seen not only in the country but also in the villages and small provincial towns. In the latter, bread was no longer bought from the baker but was baked at home in wood-burning stoves or in ovens built especially for this purpose.

In Table 2 we see that few ovens were constructed in the 1940s, but that there was an increase in the 1950s. We learned from our informants that the cost of chemical fertilizers and farming equipment, which had become increasingly important at that time, made it necessary to save money in other areas. This may seem a strange reason for building an oven. It is true that many housewives used their stove ovens, but the excessive heat caused by baking four or five batches on the same day forced some to use an outdoor oven for bread baking. The problem of baking the twenty or so large loaves required weekly was solved by the outdoor oven, which could bake them all at once. The bread oven is therefore closely connected with the family diet,[114] and as long as bread remains the most important food, the use of this oven to bake it in permits a significant saving and ensures a better organization of household tasks.

Finally, we should say a few words about the ovens that we have grouped under the name of "summer ovens". They are all located outdoors and include ovens that are used only occasionally during the summer, either for personal needs or to make a little extra money during the tourist season. We have also included in this category several ornamental ovens that have never been used for cooking. All of these summer ovens seem to us to express a feeling of pride in old traditions and a need for cultural identification.

In fact, the bread oven may be considered as an element of nationalism. It is very frequently used as a characteristic symbol of the people's way of life. A look at paintings and sculptures, as well as other works of art, reveals that artists often choose the oven as a central theme. At Saint-Jean-Port-Joli for instance, the local artists offer us a wide choice of miniature ovens skilfully sculpted in wood. The sketches of Edmond-J. Massicotte and Horatio Walker or the canvases of Yves Lemelin, Blanche Bolduc, and many others often feature a woman baking bread in an oven. Also, in the Saint-Jean-Baptiste parade, the people are always proud to

Table 2

Ovens Observed during Summer 1972 Field Trip, Showing Year of Construction

| Decades | Indoor ovens | | | | Outdoor ovens | Summer ovens |
| | Buildings | | Ground floor | Cellar | | |
	Detached	Adjoining				
1970						
1960						
1950						
1940						
1930						
1920						
1910						
1900						
1890						
1880						
1870						
1860						
1850						
1840						
1830						
1820						
1810						
1800						
1790						
1780						
1770						
1760						
1750						
1740						

◨ Clay oven
◣ Brick oven
◙ Other

Clay oven with a clapboard roof-shelter;
built at Saint-Ambroise in the summer of
1971 to commemorate the past
Lac Saint-Jean
Blanchette Collection,
NMC AC-21-74-2

A Saint-Jean-Baptiste Day parade-float
with bread making as its theme
Chambord, lac Saint-Jean
Archives de la Société historique
du Saguenay, Chicoutimi

convey the importance of the old oven and batch of bread by means of an allegorical float. This practice is still in vogue today. During the summer of 1972, for example, we came across three villages that had constructed a bread oven for a special celebration—Saint-Pierre-les-Becquets for Saint-Jean-Baptiste day, Rivière-Ouelle for its tricentennial celebrations, and Saint-Séverin for its centennial.

Typological Considerations

Let us return for a moment to a number of technical and typological considerations. In the tables, we classified ovens according to their location and material. A typology of the oven should include more than that; it should take into account both the shape of the dome and its material, the type of shelter, the location of the oven, and what the oven is used for.

Of all these considerations, shape is the most important, since in the material culture, as Henry Glassie[115] so ably demonstrated, this is the most traditional characteristic; it remains the same from one place to another and from one period to the next. Thus, the inner shape of the dome always increases gradually in height, from the door to the rear of the oven. However, this elevation should be moderate, neither too high nor too low in relation to the size of the opening, so as to permit good hot-air circulation in the oven; Diderot pointed this out in his *Encyclopédie*. We wanted to check the variability of this factor in the ovens constructed in Quebec. In order to do so, we calculated what we shall call the index of circulation, using the information in our technical data, which gave the exact external and internal dimensions of the ovens. Taking the maximum internal height of the dome as 100, this index represents the part of the dome that rises above the height of the opening. It is obtained by the following formula:

$$\frac{\text{internal height of the dome} - \text{height of the opening}}{\text{internal height of the dome}} \times 100$$

In this way we found that the average index of circulation in all the ovens we examined was 37. In other words, the average oven had a dome measuring 100 units in height and an opening measuring 63; therefore the dome was 37 units higher than the height of the opening. We then took this further. After noting that one-third of the ovens had a draft hole at the rear, we wondered if this indicated that an old technique had been lost, and, if so, to what degree. It would appear, in fact, that the technique of forming the traditional shape has been lost, as has people's confidence in it. According to the old people we spoke to, the real oven builders took care to give the dome the correct elevation and thus did not have to make a hole in it.[116] We checked these statements mathematically by plotting on a graph the circulation indexes of ovens both with and without holes. The results show a pronounced curve for the ovens without holes and a wavy line with a crest at each end for those with holes. We therefore have an

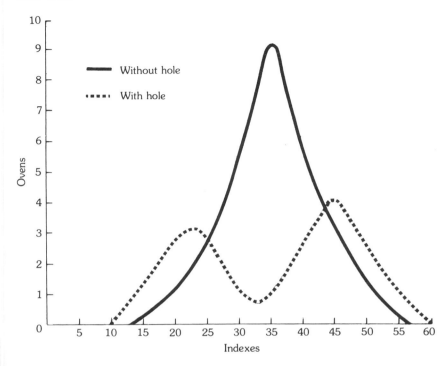

average index of 36 for ovens without holes and two indexes for ovens with holes, one lower than 23 and one higher than 45. Although fewer than one hundred ovens were studied to establish this curve, we can assume that a hole was necessary for ovens with too little or too much elevation.

The outer shape of the ovens depends on the materials available. Brick domes always have the same unvaried shape. Clay ovens allow an alternative—the dome may be continuous from the door to the back of the oven, or it may be interrupted by a ridge over the door. This ridge probably came into being with the appearance of doors having a wide ledge around the door frame. A stone structure is sometimes used to protect the oven; this gives it a different appearance but does not change the shape of the dome itself.

Outdoor ovens sometimes have shelters that are slanted towards the back of the oven, and are thus similar to those used for semi-indoor ovens. Their height is functional, as these roofs provide a place to hang meat for smoking and serve as a shelter when a batch of loaves is put in the oven. As for the shapes of other roofs, we were unable to discover the reasons for their variability.

The location of the ovens varies greatly. Neither our archival research nor our fieldwork indicated any geographical concentration; both indoor and outdoor ovens are found in all the regions studied. As for

their date of origin, the archival records are still too sketchy to allow us to determine when there was a concentration of a given type of oven.

In the study conducted during the summer of 1972, we attempted to relate the utilization of the ovens to their location on rural land. A careful examination of the data leads us to assume that these two factors—physical location and utilization—have a direct connection with the socio-economic organization of country life. We have attempted to demonstrate the interrelationship of these various aspects by showing how the oven is linked to other culinary and domestic activities.

The Oven Builders

The construction of bread ovens requires a precise technique that only a good craftsman is able to master. Oven building is more a craft than a trade. In general, brick ovens are the only ones built by skilled workers— bricklayers. Their construction does not give rise to the abundance of celebrations, linguistic expressions, and metaphors that surround the building of clay ovens. For every term or expression related to brick ovens, there may be ten for clay ovens.

The building of a clay oven calls for a true craftsman. He may be a specialist in oven building, known either locally or throughout the region; such a man was Alexis, called Le Trotteur, whose reputation lives in the memories of the people of the Saguenay–Lac-Saint-Jean and Charlevoix regions. In some areas, people remember where certain oven builders used to live: in Baie-Sainte-Catherine, they speak of Motté Dufour; in Chambord, Onésime Laforêt, nicknamed "Beau Poil"; in Pointe-Bleue, "Léon des Bonnes Âmes"; in Saint-Charles-Borromée, Alexis Bradette; in Saint-Henri-de-Taillon, Ernest Tremblay; in Saint-Urbain, the brothers Élie and François Lavoie; and so on.

In addition, there are all the anonymous craftsmen who know how to work the clay with care, who discover its special qualities, and who create objects that come alive. The technical knowledge possessed by farmers easily enables them to become good oven builders, and they are eager to describe, in their own colourful language, how they use the various materials. They provided us with a wealth of comparisons, expressions and cultural manifestations pertaining to the existence of the bread oven.

The vocabulary used is taken from daily life. These ovens and the process of building them give rise to particularly expressive forms of speech: "People . . . also like to use striking images in their conversation, metaphors that reinforce the expression of their ideas."[117] The craftsmen who build clay ovens are always making comparisons with the various things they see around them. Because of their concrete vocabulary, they turn to metaphors taken from their intimate knowledge of nature and from their own experience. Thus, they would say that the task of packing down the clay is like the work of swallows building their nest.[118] The craftsmen who shape the oven continually compare the working of the clay to bread making; they handle the clay as if it were bread dough, and speak of

An oven-builder, Polycarpe Bouchard
Marius Barbeau Collection, 1937,
NMC 83519

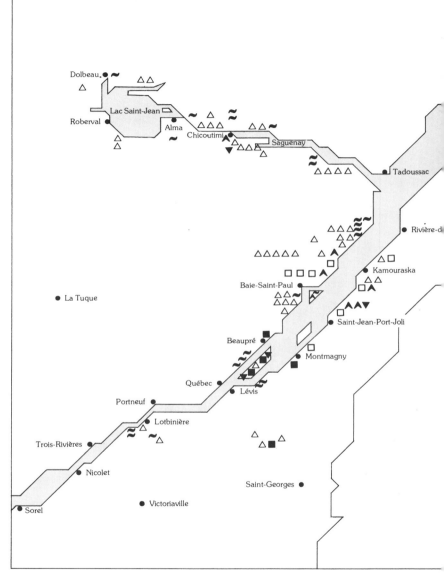

Dolbeau
Lac Saint-Jean
Roberval
Alma
Chicoutimi
Saguenay
Tadoussac
Rivière-d
Kamouraska
Baie-Saint-Paul
La Tuque
Saint-Jean-Port-Joli
Beaupré
Montmagny
Québec
Lévis
Portneuf
Lotbinière
Trois-Rivières
Nicolet
Saint-Georges
Victoriaville
Sorel

42

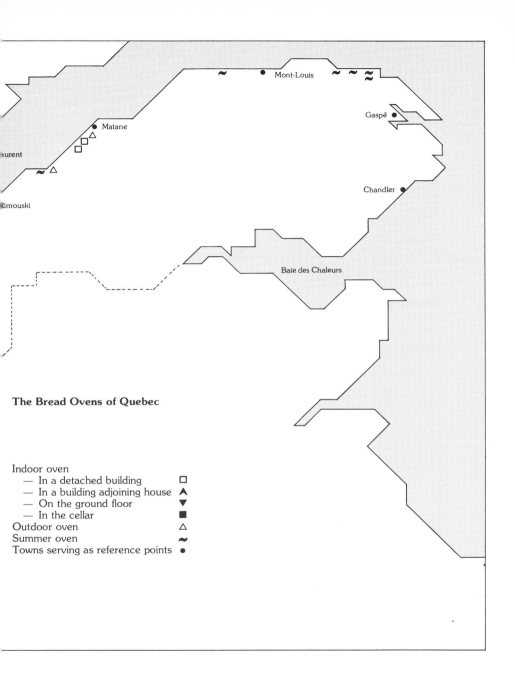

The Bread Ovens of Quebec

Indoor oven
  — In a detached building ☐
  — In a building adjoining house ▲
  — On the ground floor ▼
  — In the cellar ■
Outdoor oven △
Summer oven ~
Towns serving as reference points ●

"loaves" of clay. They say that the oven itself looks like a large loaf of bread.[119] They describe the parts of the oven as parts of living beings, speaking of the oven's legs, skeleton, carcass, flanks, hips, back, belly, paunch, rump, and mouth. They even go so far as to say that "the oven vomits, or throws up, when smoke escapes through its doors".[120]

The construction of a clay oven also gives rise to spontaneous celebrations and activities—singsongs, dances, children's games, the modelling of symbolic animals on the clay ridge of the oven, and even the "baptism" of the oven.

In describing the unsurpassed skill of Alexis, Félix-Antoine Savard related the excitement and joy that surrounded the work of this craftsman: "Mud-spattered children clapped their hands", and as soon as the first baking proved the quality of the oven, "there was endless dancing and merrymaking."[121] Children would imitate the work of the craftsman by making little clay loaves and even miniature ovens that could cook just as well as the real ones.[122] Our informant told us that when he was very young, about eight or nine years old, he made himself a small clay oven with a wooden base and an alder-branch frame. His mother placed small balls of dough, made especially for him, in sardine cans, and the baking was as successful as in the large oven.[123] But all this was only part of the greater joy expressed by families as they celebrated their new oven by "baptizing" it. The oven was appropriately toasted all round and blessed by a local priest,[124] and friends and neighbours were invited to a party to mark the joyous event.[125]

The animal theme so often used in Quebec handicraft also appears on clay ovens. Some craftsmen sculpted small clay animals on the ridge of the oven as a decoration or finishing touch, or even simply to amuse the children:

In the old days our craftsmen were sufficiently interested in the animal world around them to draw inspiration from it as well as to use various themes that were often both striking and amusing.[126]

In Charlevoix and Saguenay the duck and beaver are used. Alexis le Trotteur amused himself by sculpting these animals on the ridge of his ovens,[127] and other Charlevoix craftsmen used the figure of a duck, which supposedly watched over the various comings and goings to and from the oven.[128] These symbolic animals are smashed during the "baptism", when the oven is used for the first time. For this reason, only traces of the sculpted figures can now be seen on the collars of bread ovens, as in the drawings at the bottom of page 23.

This animal theme also finds expression in the comparison of the dome of the oven to a crouching beaver,[129] once again confirming that "in the popular imagination, the animal world constituted a huge reservoir of metaphorical terminology."[130]

Chapter II

The Construction of a Clay Bread Oven beside the Rivière à Mars

During the summer of 1971, we had the opportunity to observe the construction of a clay bread oven. The experience of watching this family task and the images we retained of the event prompted us to write the following description of the technique, the craftsman, and his work.

The art of shaping a clay bread oven reveals the skill of the self-made craftsman. From a little clay he shapes an object to meet his needs. We hope to convey the full significance of this act by describing the construction of a bread oven according to the method of an experienced farmer from the Saguenay region, Mr. Louis-Joseph Simard. He agreed to make the oven because he believes that the techniques he learned in his youth are worth recording for future generations. After explaining the method he used thirty-five years ago, he gave us a full practical demonstration.

The construction of this oven took place on the campground of the parish of Saint-Marc at Bagotville on 22 and 23 June 1971. The site is located on the banks of the Rivière à Mars[1] in the Saint-Pierre concession of Bagotville. From the choice of site, we could see that all the necessary materials would be on hand, and all that remained was for the craftsman to select them with his experienced eye.

Mr. Simard was closely assisted by his son-in-law, Mr. Lauréat Lévesque, and there was also active participation by several members of the family and by young people from the campground. According to Mr. Simard, this job is meant to be a family event, with all the members of the family providing mutual encouragement until the completion of the work. Mr. Simard was born at the turn of the century and learned to make bread ovens in his youth from his grandfather, Johnny Simard, who had learned the technique in Baie-Saint-Paul, where he lived. Louis-Joseph Simard is a master of his grandfather's method, having built a number of ovens under his guidance as well as constructing others by himself. He made the last one thirty-five years ago; it was later used at the first Chicoutimi Winter Carnival. Mr. Simard first described the method to us and then proceeded to demonstrate it. The original technique remains the same, except for the use of cement instead of the old mortar made of lime and sand.

The oven is made up of various distinct parts that differ in shape and in the material used. The oven consists of the base, which provides a foundation for the hearth, then the doors, the dome, and, finally, the shelter that protects the whole thing. The construction will take a full day's work, and all the necessary materials have been brought to the site.

47

Base

To ensure the solidity and durability of the oven, weather-resistant materials are selected to make the platform. Mr. Simard chooses stones from the river to build a strong foundation. First he levels the earth and marks out a rectangle measuring 75 by 47 inches (1.9 by 1.2 m). He then lays the largest stones around the perimeter of this rectangle and places the medium-sized stones inside. Next he pours sand into the gaps. He gradually builds up this base by adding other stones to the perimeter and to the inside of the rectangle, again pouring sand between the stones, until the base measures 16 inches (40.6 cm) in height. Sand used in this way acts as a buffer and insulator between the hearth and the ground. The next step is to mix the cement in a trough situated near the oven site and to pour it over the foundation. With all the spaces filled and the stones held firmly together, the platform is solid and stable and is now ready to support the other massive parts of the oven.

Hearth

The hearth, "the part on which the dome of the oven rests",[2] is the first section laid on this platform. Since it is on this horizontal surface—the actual oven floor—that the loaves of bread are placed for baking, special care is taken to ensure that it is as smooth as possible.

Mr. Simard told us that thirty-five years ago he used bricks to make the hearth, but now he uses cement. In order to determine the exact size of the hearth, he makes a rectangular frame, using boards that he lays directly on the stones of the platform. He fits it firmly in place, inserting underneath it two projecting "two-by-fours", one near the front and the other towards the rear, to be used later as a support for the shelter. Next, he prepares a large batch of cement that he pours inside the frame right up to the edge, giving the hearth a thickness of four inches, actually $3\frac{5}{8}$ inches (9.2 cm)—the wider dimension of the two-by-four. He then levels off this mortar lightly, and immediately fits on the oven doors.

Doors

The doors facilitate the positioning of the frame, hold the alder branches in place, and close off the mouth of the oven. Doors with an inward-sloping ledge were used in this oven; their ledge held one end of the alder branches making up the frame and supported the masonry forming the mouth of the oven. Above the double doors was the partially worn inscription, BERNIER.

The doors play a key role in the rest of the construction, and Mr. Simard inserts them into the front end of the hearth. He places the sill in the cement, thus ensuring that the doors will be solidly attached once the cement hardens. Using a trowel, he finishes smoothing off the surface of the hearth, eliminating any unevenness. To give the base and hearth time to set, he waits until the next day before erecting the rest of the oven.

Large stones are used to make the base
Lise and Jean-François Blanchette Collection

The doorsill is placed in front of the
hearth
Lise and Jean-François Blanchette Collection

Cutting and preparing young branches
for the framework
Lise and Jean-François Blanchette Collection

Framework

At dawn the following day, Mr. Simard begins cutting the alder branches. With a sure step, he leads the way to an alder grove at the end of his property. There he measures the branches and tests them for flexibility. With his axe he cuts down those which appear the most suitable, some long and some short. He then trims them, ties them together in bundles, and carries them on his back to the barn, where he picks up a few tools and a bale of hay. We then proceed to the oven site.

He checks to see that the cement of the hearth has hardened sufficiently and begins to mark off the correct size for the dome, telling us that in the old days bread pans were used to determine the correct size. Since he has not brought any pans, Mr. Simard makes a guide of crossed pieces of wood, wide at the back and narrowing towards the doors, and lays it on the floor of the hearth. Around them is laid a wooden form to mark out the size of the dome and secure the alder branches. Traditionally, when the hearth was made of clay, this form was not needed, and when the hearth was made of brick, enough room was left for the tips of the branches. But here the use of cement causes a slight problem in that the ends of the alder branches cannot be inserted in it.

The frame is a type of scaffolding, made of alder and hazel branches, upon which the dome of the oven is built. It is this frame that determines the shape of the dome. It can also be regarded as a support or arch on which the lumps of clay are laid. However, there is more to it than this, and a closer examination reveals that its simple, rustic style requires considerable skill on the part of the craftsman as well as intimate knowledge of the materials used. The craftsman has to work quickly to position all the pieces of wood before they dry and harden. Mr. Simard's method involves making the shape of the frame larger and rounder than other methods, and higher at the back than at the front. When the oven is completed, this shape facilitates hot-air circulation at the back of the oven and makes for a more even heating of the dome. Moreover, it gives more strength to the framework.

Sometimes it is necessary to strip one side of the alder and hazel branches in order to make them flexible enough. Alder wood is preferred to hazel because it is stronger and easier to work with. In fact, the craftsman will use only two or three hazel branches for the frame.

With the help of his son-in-law, Mr. Simard begins constructing the framework. Taking a large alder branch, he works it with his hands along its entire length to make it more flexible; then, holding it against his knee, he bends it to the desired curve. He nails one of the ends to the back of the wooden guide, positions the alder branch over the centre of the hearth, and brings the other end over to the mouth of the oven. To keep the alder branch at the right height and angle, he places a wooden plank vertically towards the rear of the oven to support the branch and to retain its arched position. Taking a second alder branch, he works it in the same way as the first and positions it towards the back and crosswise over the first branch. The builders then check to see that the first two alder

The first alder branches are put in place
Lise and Jean-François Blanchette Collection

Positioning the long alder branches
Lise and Jean-François Blanchette Collection

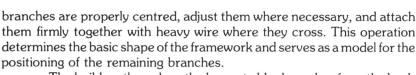

branches are properly centred, adjust them where necessary, and attach them firmly together with heavy wire where they cross. This operation determines the basic shape of the framework and serves as a model for the positioning of the remaining branches.

The builders then place the longest alder branches from the back of the oven to the front, and complete the framework lengthwise by adding seven more branches, which are positioned on each side of the first branch. The same procedure is repeated: stripping the branch with the axe, working and bending it with the hands and knees, placing one of the ends at the back of the wooden guide, bending it to the correct angle, positioning the outer end at the mouth, and finally attaching it with wire to secure the shape. Care is taken to maintain the proper balance between the length and the height of the dome.

Once the operation is completed, the next step is to add the remaining alder branches crosswise. For this, the craftsmen use the small alders that are left over, but since there are not enough of them, Mr. Lévesque fells severals hazel trees alongside the river. The technique used is the same as for the length of the frame. They place the seven alder and hazel branches in front of and behind the first transverse alder branch, positioning them directly over the longer branches in order to reinforce the framework. In this way, Mr. Simard and Mr. Lévesque firmly position all the alder branches over the whole length of the frame, attaching them with wire at each crossover point. This method gives the framework the strength and solidity needed to support the heavy weight of the lumps of clay.

The frame is thus completed. The rear part is slightly more prominent than the front. The craftsmen remove the wooden form that was used to mark out the periphery of the frame when the alder branches were positioned. Mr. Simard cleans the surface of the hearth with a small broom made of leaves and put together especially for that purpose, and turns towards us with a grin, saying, "As you can see, nature provides everything we need."

Dome

The construction of the dome is a fascinating process. This is the mud-walling stage during which the craftsmen mould and shape the clay "like swallows building their nests", to use Mr. Simard's expression. Kneading together clay mixed with hay, they shape blocks of the mixture, which they place over each joint of the framework to give stability to the dome. A number of different steps are involved in making the blocks of clay, including the preparation and assembly of all the required items near the oven site—a rectangular trough, weathered clay, a shovel, pails, loose hay, and two small benches made of rough planks.

The clay used came from the clay hills across from Baie des Ha! Ha! It was transported to the campground the previous summer and allowed to weather. The expression "weathered clay" refers to dried clay that has contracted in the winter cold and therefore pulls apart easily; the

Positioning the transverse alder
branches
Lise and Jean-François Blanchette Collection

The framework reveals the eventual
shape of the oven
Lise and Jean-François Blanchette Collection

more weathered the clay the more manageable it becomes. This particular clay was greatly appreciated by our craftsmen.

Our septuagenarian then starts to work the clay, demonstrating his own particular brand of humour. Evoking the memory of Alexis le Trotteur, he challenges the young people on the campsite to "dance up a storm" in order to pound the clay to the right consistency. The laughter and the first sounds of feet stomping in the trough augur well. For the young people, dancing takes on a new dimension—they now have a challenge to meet.

Several shovelfuls of earth are placed in the trough along with some water. The barefoot dancers stomp and pound the clay-and-water mixture until a smooth consistency is obtained. The craftsmen place a good-sized handful of hay on one of the benches. They then take a chunk of wet clay from the trough, and with firm and energetic movements they knead together the hay and clay to remove any excess water and to obtain the right consistency. The hay acts as a binding material and reinforces the oven; it must be thoroughly mixed in with the clay. The craftsmen know this and work hard to complete their task successfully. Next, they skilfully lift up the prepared blocks and begin to place them on the front part of the frame. The first blocks are positioned on the hearth so as to make the lower part of the wall very thick; the sides of the dome must be extremely strong to support the weight of the other clay blocks.

While the dancers continue to mix the clay and water, the craftsmen scoop out another chunk of wet clay, mix in some hay with their large hands and begin the kneading process again. They work the clay as if it were bread dough—the more they handle it the better the texture will be. Returning to the front of the hearth, they place the new blocks of clay above the first row, following the ledge of the door-frame.

With mounting excitement at seeing the oven take shape before their eyes, the dancers continue to trample in the trough, while Mr. Simard and Mr. Lévesque shape the blocks of clay. As soon as each block is ready, they place it at the front of the frame, building up a clay ridge, or collar, just above the doors. Already there is a difference between the walls of the dome and the collar of the oven. The walls are as much as 9 or 10 inches (23 or 25 cm) thick near the hearth, and decrease in thickness towards the upper part of the dome. This creates a balanced construction and keeps in the heat as long as possible.

In spite of the overwhelming heat of the noonday sun, the work goes on. The dancers continue to trample and tread on the clay, the craftsmen keep on kneading the clay and hay. The work requires the sustained effort of the arms, the hands, and indeed the entire body. The blocks of clay are lined up side by side on the curved alder branches. They are pushed together and lightly smoothed by hand. Sometimes a little water is added to the surface.

The work is progressing at a frantic pace by now, and the workers are constantly surveying the oven as it takes shape before their eyes. Soon, the hump of the dome begins to appear. The craftsmen stand back to see if the clay mass is well balanced. Working along the length of the

frame towards the back of the oven, they make sure that the blocks of clay placed on the hearth are thick enough and that those making up the upper part of the dome are tapered.

To speed up the work, they put the straw directly into the trough while Mrs. Louis-Philippe Simard and Mrs. Eugène Girard help to form the blocks of clay. The work begins to take on the appearance of a family celebration, and everyone is happy to take part.

The craftsmen continue applying clay blocks to the rear of the oven. The beautifully smooth shape, the roundness of the dome, is clearly apparent. The frame is almost completely covered with clay, and only a small part of the alder-branch trelliswork can be seen. Slowly but surely the rear of the oven is covered up, and the last clay blocks are put solidly into place. With a satisfied grin, Mr. Lévesque applies the last clay block as shouts of joy are heard from the participants and spectators, who are already dreaming of the first batch of bread.

However, the job is not completely finished. With their large hands covered with bits of clay,[3] the craftsmen smooth down all the clay blocks to obtain the correct shape and, dipping their hands in water, they glaze the entire clay surface. A few strands of straw stick out here and there.

The oven has become a reality, and, to use the delightful expression of Félix-Antoine Savard, "the fire urn"[4] is now ready for the first firing.

Shelter

To prevent erosion of the materials, a triangular shelter is constructed to protect the oven from the weather. The shelter is very simply built, and is basically a clapboard roof over the dome extending down to the foundation.

Mr. Lévesque now removes the planks that were used as a framework for the hearth. Only the ends of the two beams emerge from the sides of the hearth. On these beams he erects the rafters that rise above the dome to the cross-brace. Then, on the wooden frame he places a row of aspen planks followed by a row of battens. He completes the roof of the shelter by putting on the ridge cap. The shelter at no point touches the masonry of the dome.

Drying and Firing the Oven

The oven will be left to dry in the air for at least eight days before the first firing in order to permit evaporation of the water in the clay. Every day a few new cracks will appear on the dome and will be repaired immediately. On the eighth day, a small fire is laid to burn out the alder-branch framework and to begin hardening the dome slowly. Successive firings will further harden the oven.

The "dancers" pound the clay and water
together with their feet
Lise and Jean-François Blanchette Collection

Mr. Simard shaping a "loaf" of clay
Lise and Jean-François Blanchette Collection

The craftsman mixes hay into the clay
Lise and Jean-François Blanchette Collection

Shaping the blocks of clay
Lise and Jean-François Blanchette Collection

The side walls are made very thick
Lise and Jean-François Blanchette Collection

The door-frame determines the shape of
the collar, or ridge
Lise and Jean-François Blanchette Collection

The clay blocks are laid around the arch
of the doors
Lise and Jean-François Blanchette Collection

Every member of the family participates!
Lise and Jean-François Blanchette Collection

Checking to see that the oven is well
shaped
Lise and Jean-François Blanchette Collection

The bare framework begins to disappear
under the clay vault
Lise and Jean-François Blanchette Collection

Mrs. Louis-Philippe Simard kneads a
block of clay while Mr. Lévesque checks
the walls
Lise and Jean-François Blanchette Collection

The dome is gradually sealed
Lise and Jean-François Blanchette Collection

Positioning the last clay blocks
Lise and Jean-François Blanchette Collection

The craftsmen seal the last joints
Lise and Jean-François Blanchette Collection

Mr. Lévesque smoothes and seals the
collar
Lise and Jean-François Blanchette Collection

From the side the oven resembles a
crouching beaver
Lise and Jean-François Blanchette Collection

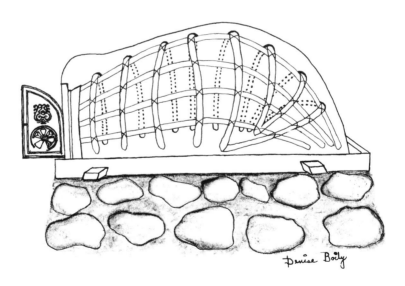

The various parts of the oven, showing
the base, the framework and the final
shape
Drawing by Denise Boily
Blanchette Collection, CCFCS Archives

Building the shelter
Lise and Jean-François Blanchette Collection

70

Nailing on the battens
Lise and Jean-François Blanchette Collection

Putting the ridge cap in place
Lise and Jean-François Blanchette Collection

71

The "fire urn" is ready for the first batch
of loaves
Lise and Jean-François Blanchette Collection

Chapter III

The Bread

Bread making seems a simple task. One might naively believe that it is merely a repeated and almost magical interaction between the heat and the dough. However, in the bread-making process there is a special relationship between the various natural products and the baker who uses them skilfully. We have only to consider the care that must be given in regulating the heat, selecting the ingredients, and using the correct handling techniques. All the older women who have been baking all their lives, and continue to do so, constantly reminded us throughout our study that baking a successful batch of bread is almost an art. Bread, that "sacred" food of our ancestors, that "food rolled into a ball, full of air holes, lopsided, sour or sweet, oval or round, soft or hard, black or white, that staff of life"[1] remains a subject of great interest.

We shall study, step by step, the procedure for making this precious food, examining the different flours and leavening agents used and the various types of bread that result. We shall attempt to explain the difference between the so-called *habitant* bread and the bread we use today, which one of our informants says tastes little better than whitewash.[2]

Bread making, or the practical knowledge of how to transform flour into bread, can be divided into well-defined phases. These are the kneading of the dough, the fermentation or rising of the dough, and, finally, the baking that produces the actual bread and turns the loaves a golden colour. Flour, yeast, water, salt, fat, and sometimes sugar are the main ingredients. We will remain faithful to the recipes of our informants, who have produced this staple food countless times. We will also refer occasionally to two important works published by the Quebec Department of Agriculture, *La grande erreur du pain blanc*, published in 1916,[3] and *Le pain de ménage*, published in 1934, with a new edition in 1940.[4] The first of these pamphlets points out the harmful consequences of not using natural bread and advocates its return. The second attempts to encourage "more actively the campaign already under way to promote the use of home-grown flour and the baking of bread in the home".[5] It also encourages greater self-sufficiency on the farm: "This campaign . . . is a very timely one, since the current depression forces everyone to make the most of everything in order to make ends meet."[6] It is therefore not surprising to find instructions for constructing clay and brick ovens, as well as a number of recipes.

Grains and Flours

Flour is the prime ingredient for making bread. Its texture, lightness, and colour indicate the quality of the bread that can be made from it. Rural people used all types of flour. The choice depended on many factors—the region in question, the soil, the climate, periods of economic crisis, blights that destroyed the harvests, and, more recently, the influence of advertising that urged people to use the well-known white flour made available by the new industrial processes.

If we look at the history of New France, we can grasp the impact of the need for bread-making flour on the survival of the people and on the economy of the times. The importance of flour is reflected in the obligations of the Compagnie des Cent-Associés with respect to the distribution of wheat to the first colonists: "Wheat was the most indispensable element of life. This was true for all the French people of that time. Bread was the very basis of their nutrition."[7] Wheat was regarded as the grain that would give people the energy they required. Jean Hamelin, in his study entitled *Économie et Société en Nouvelle-France*, points out the prime importance of wheat to the colony:

> The crucial role of wheat can be explained by the fact that Canadians of the time, together with their brothers in France, were great consumers of bread. "Each labourer", writes the author of the *Relation* of 1636, "eats two six- or seven-pound loaves a week." Raudot maintained in 1716 that "the colonist consumes two pounds of bread and six ounces of lard per day." Bread is therefore the most fundamental element on which the nutrition of the people is based.[8]

At first, "wooden or stone mortars were used"[9] to mill this grain, but gradually flour mills were introduced. In 1685, there were 41 flour mills in all of Canada, but by 1734 the number had reached 118.[10] Even though wheat seems to have been the preferred grain for making bread in past centuries, it is clear that in periods of scarcity and poor harvests the French pioneers must certainly have used other grains to make their flour. Originally they had all come from a country where other grains had long been used: "With regard to grains, wheat is always the best, followed by mixed wheat and rye, then rye and barley, and finally oats, peas, and vetch."[11] This quotation indicates that the first colonists must have turned to grains other than wheat to make flour for their bread. For example, if we look at the period preceding the British conquest, we find that a famine forced the people to take advantage of what little they had: "22 November 1756 . . . Since it has been a very bad year, we are mixing peas with the flour to make the bread, a quart of peas to a quart of flour."[12] The following quotation removes any possible doubt: "The poor farmers ate bread made of pea flour, a supremely indigestible kind of food."[13] We should also note that, around 1850, bread made of barley flour was used in the Saguenay:

> The fertility of the country around lac Saint-Jean is seen in the fact that in Chicoutimi a farmer ate barley bread made from the year's harvest.[14]

The cook carefully watches for signs
that it is time to begin the baking
Public Archives of Canada,
no. C-21266

Agility and skill are required to manip-
ulate the long-handled tools
Public Archives of Canada,
no. C-21270

In the twentieth century, there is a wide variety of crops suitable for making bread—wheat, barley, rye, buckwheat, oats, corn, and certain types of beans.

Wheat is the ideal grain because it contains "all the major food components, including starch, albumin, fats, and minerals."[15] Not all Quebec farmers grow wheat. In some regions the growing season is too short, and in others wheat will not grow at all. It is important to select the right grain:

> Only two varieties of wheat can be grown here with any success. They not only ripen early, but also have good baking qualities. They are as follows: 1—Marquis wheat: productive, fairly early, excellent baking qualities; . . . 2—Garnet wheat: productive, very early . . . good baking qualities. . . . It is suitable for northern regions.[16]

Some of our informants frequently recalled the way things used to be. They grew the wheat and then milled the grain to obtain *habitant* flour for making whole-wheat bread. They insisted on their preference for wheat flour. With it they made *habitant* bread, highly nutritious, brown in colour, with an almond-like flavour. The quality of wheat flour had deteriorated with the progressive development of milling techniques, from the original millstone method to the more modern mills using new industrial processes in the second half of the nineteenth century. The mills quickly succumbed to industrialization; the old millstones were put away to make room for metal rollers. The quality of the flour gradually degenerated, ushering in the era of the infamous white bread.[17] Brown whole-wheat flour gave way to white flour, which was considered to be a "nutritional mistake". White flour replaced "whole and unsifted flour, [which] has few nutrients, lacks minerals, phosphorus, and digestible wheats, and, moreover, is constipating".[18] Nevertheless, pure whole-wheat flour went out of general use.

However, wheat was not the only grain to produce bread-making flour. Milled barley was often used for family needs, especially when the stocks of wheat had run out.[19] This grain needed more milling than wheat and produced a black bread that was chewy and tough.[20]

Rye is easier to cultivate than wheat and grows quickly. It produces a brown, heavy bread that is more difficult to digest.[21] Sometimes a mixture of wheat flour and rye flour was used in order to make the wheat flour last longer, especially when the family was large and there was not enough wheat flour from the last harvest. There were other reasons for adding rye:

> Frequently a small amount of rye is added to wheat flour for two reasons: 1—It is believed that this keeps the bread fresh longer. 2—The rye gives a special flavour to the bread.[22]

Buckwheat was also milled to obtain the gluten. People cultivated this black wheat, which grew in most soils and in almost all climates. Buckwheat flour satisfied many tastes, though it was more compact than wheat flour and browner and more dense as well. It produced a heavy bread, one that was very chewy, with very small air holes that looked as black as the grain itself.[23]

A number of our informants spoke of oat flour, but since this grain gives too much bran, its use was rather restricted. The people of Saint-Justin made a mixture of wheat and corn: "The bread is made from wheat flour to which a little corn flour is sometimes added to make the bread more crumbly."[24] We were also told of the use of a kind of bean that was ground up for making bread.[25]

Finally, we wish to stress that the quality of the flour is extremely important:

> The baking quality of wheat depends upon the ability of the dough to trap the gas resulting from fermentation. This property depends upon the gluten. Not all grains are of equal baking quality. Grains that are good for making porridge, such as sorghum, buckwheat, corn, oats and rice, are poor in gluten and produce a very heavy bread. Rye produces flour that can be used for making bread, but it is inferior to wheat flour. . . . Wheat is the very best grain for making bread.[26]

To sum up, we can say that, for the past century and longer, the use of bread-making flours in French-Canadian kitchens is related to such diverse factors as climate, the type of soil, the standard of living, the particular tastes of country people, and the advertising to promote the use of white flour.

Leavening Agents

Since the fermentation process is of prime importance in bread making, it is necessary to describe the leaven, the ingredient that activates the dough and makes it ready for baking. First, what does "rising", or fermentation, mean and what is its role? The answer to this will help us to understand certain facts. Fermentation "involves a process that changes the starch into dextrin, the dextrin into glucose, and the glucose in turn into alcohol and carbon dioxide. It is the release of numerous bubbles of carbon dioxide that makes the dough rise and creates air holes in the bread."[27] This reaction is caused by the use of certain leavening agents.

The familiar commercially prepared yeast that appeared in the early part of the twentieth century supplanted domestic leavens by ensuring uniformly good results. With the increased use of this yeast many of the old secrets were forgotten, so that today it is not an easy matter to trace information on the almost magic formulas for the leavens used by pioneers. We did manage to track down a few rare places where the old recipes had continued to be handed down and used even after the introduction of commercial leavens. A number of those interviewed spoke to us on the subject, and various older as well as more recent documents answered other questions that occurred to us.

The first colonists who settled in New France created their leavens from the cooking techniques used in the mother country. Certain similarities between the old leavens, which were used before the advent of the yeast cake, and the leavens made in French kitchens in the eighteenth century help us to interpret our findings. Leaven "is merely raw dough that has been kept for seven or eight days and has gone sour. . . . This leaven is normally taken from the dough of the last batch of bread made, and is composed of either wheat, mixed wheat, and rye, or some other type of bread that is being prepared; it is a piece of raw dough, weighing about a pound, that ferments as it turns sour; as it does this it causes the dough with which it is combined to rise as well."[28] This old French procedure left its mark on domestic culinary practices, and we were able to uncover evidence of its influence during our study. In his history of bread, Jacques Rousseau made some very apt observations on the leaven, which he defines as "a sourdough added to fresh dough during the kneading process".[29]

The process is a simple one. The flours used for bread making contain a varying percentage of gluten, a substance that helps bread to rise. Even before the appearance of commercial yeast, therefore, it was possible to make the dough rise to the appropriate degree because of the properties of this gluten. Nevertheless, one still had to be a good baker to use the correct quantities and to choose the grain with the greatest amount of gluten.

The old ways are still keenly remembered by some of our informants. Before the commercial yeast cake arrived on the market, women kept a little raw dough from the last batch of bread and left it to sour in a small container placed near the ceiling beams in the kitchen, where it was warm. Some of them would allow this piece of dough to dry in a corner of the dough box. The dough would ferment and develop new strength for the next batch of bread. After five to eight days, this ball of dough would be soaked in lightly salted water; it would then come apart easily. A little flour would be added, and the whole would be incorporated into the new dough, thus expanding it. Occasionally this ball of dough would be borrowed by the neighbours when they had forgotten to keep back some dough from the last baking, or when there was not enough leaven for the number of loaves to be made. This exchange of leaven would provide an opportunity for friendly visits between neighbours.[30]

Our informants were not the only ones to speak of this cooking technique. A number of French-Canadian authors writing in the late nineteenth and early twentieth centuries refer to it. Briefly, this is what we found: "Once the dough is made (that is, when the flour is mixed with water), a small part of it is removed and kept aside. This is allowed to ferment for a night and a day, by which time it has become leaven; it is then used in the next day's dough."[31] Closer to our own time, Eugénie Paré wrote in 1940: "In the old days, they used to make bread with a dough leaven."[32]

Sourdough was not the only leaven used. The early pioneers were quick to take advantage of the natural substances available to them. Consequently, hops and potatoes played a significant role. Hops have long been used to flavour beer. According to Jacques Rousseau, they have been known since antiquity and were introduced to New France when it was first settled. Since the sixteenth century they have been used "as a seasoning for bread, not directly, but added to the leaven as an

infusion".[33] The hop is a hardy plant that grows easily and acts as a leavening agent. The pioneers made a "stock" using the flowers and leaves of the plant. Usually, the leaven was soaked overnight. Some people prepared it in a wooden tub that was also used for keeping butter,[34] while others made it in a special container commonly called the "stock jug", or kept it warm in a corner of the dough box reserved especially for the leaven.[35] The recipes we gathered revealed several regional variations. Very often, the leaves and flowers of the hops would be dipped in boiling water, wheat flour would be added to the resulting liquid, and the mixture would then be left to sour.[36] Sometimes water in which potatoes were boiled would be added to this mixture to make it stronger.[37]

Gradually, potatoes were added to the mixture of hops and flour. Because of its high starch content, the potato was used for its catalytic effect on the action of the leaven, which causes the lump of dough to rise. Boiled potatoes, finely mashed with or without the peel, or raw potatoes, thinly sliced or grated, were used. Some of our informants even used the potato leaven alone. They would boil the potatoes in their skins, mash them, and then let them sour and dry out. A type of mould would develop. When the time came to use this leaven, they would soak it for twelve hours in a tightly closed container.[38] Others would add to the potato mixture either sour milk or a little flour, water, and sugar.[39] The potato leaven would often be combined with hops, since this mixture gave better results. Usually, boiling potato water would be poured over the hop flowers and leaves and left to steep. The potatoes would be mashed thoroughly, with or without their skins, and the previously prepared stock would be poured over them. It was thickened with a little flour and lightly seasoned with salt and sugar. Sometimes molasses would be substituted for sugar as it activated the fermentation just as well. Some cooks would dip the hops into molasses before adding the other ingredients.[40] One of our informants volunteered the following information:

> Before the appearance of commercial yeast, our grandmothers used hops boiled up with potatoes. Once this preparation had been mashed and strained, a little flour was added to make the dough; this was then divided up into little cakes and dried, without cooking, to be used for the next baking sessions. It is believed that people referred to this mixture when they said they were going to borrow some leaven.[41]

Sometimes this leaven was used in a different form. The women would lend each other a bottle containing a liquid leaven consisting of the juice of boiled potatoes, hops, and water. When they had used part of this liquid, they immediately added some more water, and in this way the leaven was replenished in the time-honoured "stock jug". During the warmer weather, children were sent all over the countryside to borrow this mixture. Those were the good old days of the "jug of leaven".[42]

The use of the potato was to continue in the home. Even with the arrival of commercial yeasts it would be used as an aid in the rising process, and today it is still used by some cooks, who mix it in with their dough as "it makes it rise better and gives the bread a better taste."[43]

In addition to these various leavens, we also discovered the use of a certain type of buckwheat cake with fermentative properties. This was a very rudimentary leaven consisting of a mixture of buckwheat flour and a little water. These little cakes were dried by hanging them from the kitchen ceiling beams. Before each baking, two cakes were soaked in water together with some flour.[44]

It seems clear that the practical knowledge of the pioneers was more than adequate. They knew how to make the most of even the smallest gifts of nature.

The beginning of the twentieth century, however, marked a turning point in culinary techniques. About seventy years ago commercial yeast cakes appeared on the market, made possible by the advances in culinary chemistry. But was this really progress, or simply a necessary corrective measure? The sequence of events suggests that there is a direct relationship between the production of commercial leaven and the use of the new roller mills, which reduced the quality of flour. In the case of sourdough leaven, among others, we know that fermentation occurred naturally and could be put to use because of the elasticity provided by the gluten in the flour. As long as the flour retained its natural yeasts and gluten, the old homemade leavens could be used successfully. Repeated failures with the new flours, however, might have made it necessary to produce a new kind of leaven. This theory is held by some authors. We know that gluten helps dough to rise and that the percentage of gluten in flour varies. If the flour is stone-ground, almost none of its baking quality is lost. On the other hand, if roller mills are used, the grain loses some of its components, including its leavening agents. "The roller mills eliminate the leaven."[45] Moreover, "the low gluten content of commercial flours is one of the objections to roller milling."[46] Eugénie Paré adds: "Flours low in gluten produce a dough that is more likely to lie down than to rise."[47]

If the flour is of poor quality, it cannot be expected to perform well. Once its percentage of gluten is decreased and its leaven destroyed, there is no alternative but to use stronger leavening agents. The incompatibilities between technical developments and domestic practices at the beginning of the twentieth century led to the appearance of commercial yeasts.

The first yeast cakes to appear on the market were round, and they were followed a few years later by square cakes. According to our informants, these little dried lumps of yeast contained a well-proportioned mixture of hops, potatoes, and malt extract.[48] The brand name Royal was undoubtedly the most popular. The next development was yeast in block form, which could be bought from the baker. And finally came the powdered yeast we use today, which can be purchased in little packages.

Preparing the yeast cake was definitely easier and more reliable. The day before the baking was to be done, two or three cakes were soaked in warm water, together with a pinch of salt and some sugar; about two hours later, after the sugar and salt had dissolved, the mixture was thickened a little with flour, allowed to rise slightly, and a little more water and flour were added. Occasionally this leaven would be reinforced with two or three boiled and mashed potatoes. It was believed that potatoes helped the bread retain its moisture.[49] The use of potatoes was optional, however, as was the addition of fat. Some of our informants had pleasant memories of the preparation of the yeast cake. Here is what one of them had to say about it:

> At suppertime my mother prepared two Royal cakes with water, sugar, salt, four or five mashed potatoes, and the water used to boil them in. When she had mixed everything together, and the sugar and salt had dissolved, she added a little flour before going to bed. This was left to rise overnight.[50]

In some homes, the container holding the leaven was placed on top of the hot-water tank on the wood stove to keep it at the correct temperature all night long. The yeast cake enjoyed widespread popularity and was even used by amateur beer-makers, who used it to improve their home brew.[51]

Preparing the Dough

The bread is made in the dough box,[52] a large wooden container with a lid; it is slightly narrower at the bottom than at the top and rests on four legs. It may be made of pine, cherry, or fir. The dough box was used for a very long time, and was kept in the kitchen even after the appearance of kneading machines. The most common model is divided into two sections inside, one used for keeping the leaven in and the other the flour.[53] However, a bin with a single trough is also often used. In some places we found a type of "table-trough", a sort of box on legs with a tray-like round cover that can be leaned against the wall. After the dough is kneaded, the tray is flipped down, and the top can be used as a dining table.[54] Along similar lines, there is the "baker's chair", equipped with arms and a backrest that, when lowered, forms a kneading table; with the back raised it becomes a very useful piece of furniture in the home.[55] Some dough boxes are equipped with a small drawer in which the dough leaven is left to sour. Occasionally, at the bottom of these containers, there is a closed cupboard where the batch of baked bread can be stored.[56] These variations of the dough box continued to be used until the arrival of kneading machines at the beginning of the twentieth century. The new blade-equipped devices made the task of kneading easier and saved precious time as well. There are various models available, some operated manually, others electrically powered.

With this great variety of technical aids, baking bread remains a subject of considerable interest. The transformation of flour, water, and leaven has always held a fascination for people, even for those who are bakers by trade and who are the only ones to be happy when they are *dans le pétrin*.[57]* A brief look at the traditional method of baking will enable us to better appreciate the work that goes into a successful batch and the laborious nature of this household chore. Incidentally, the dough was always blessed by making the sign of the cross over it.[58]

---

*Translator's note: This is a play on words. The French expression means "to be in trouble", but its literal sense is "to be in the dough box".

Failure to keep a close watch over the
state of the dough and the temperature
of the oven can be disastrous
Marius Barbeau Collection,
NMC 83536

The first step is to prepare the leaven. Next, some flour and a
pinch of salt are put in the dough box, which is placed near the stove in
winter in order to warm up the flour slightly. When the leaven and flour are
ready, an indentation is made in the flour and the leaven is poured in.
Then, with her fingers, the baker carefully incorporates some flour into
the leaven, taking care not to "smother" the mixture. A little warm water is
gradually added until a firm consistency is obtained; care must be taken
not to "drown the dough".[59] The dough is lifted up lightly and worked in
the dough box in a figure-eight pattern. In this way, air is incorporated into
the dough, which gradually swells in size. The dough is kneaded until it no
longer sticks, and is uniform and elastic. It is then left to rise for the first
time for about an hour. It is kneaded once again and left to rise a second
time to its full capacity, that is, to double its volume. Finally, the dough is
placed on the lightly floured working surface of the dough box and is
kneaded with the palms of the hands until it makes a squeaking sound.

The last step is to turn it and shape it into loaves. It rises again for the last time until ready to be put into the oven.

Throughout these operations it is of the utmost importance to avoid any drafts and to maintain a constant temperature in the room. "I remember when Dad had finished working the dough, he would make a little sign of the cross over it, and cover it up carefully so that it would not catch cold (very important so that the yeast keeps its full strength)."[60] In winter, it is necessary to compensate for the cold by raising the temperature of the house; the warmer the house the faster and higher the bread rises. To speed up the process, some women placed a boiling kettle in the side of the dough box that was not being used.

When the baker had finished shaping the loaves, they would be placed either in pans greased with salt-pork rind or simply on a wooden board powdered with flour. To amuse the children, mothers would often make little dough-men or miniature loaves.[61] These would rise and bake in sardine cans or baking-powder tins, and would be placed in the oven alongside the household bread. While the dough was rising for the last time, the fire would be lighted. Everyone preferred the taste of bread baked in those old ovens to that of any other bread, and they were very willing to stand by for the correct oven temperature, keeping an eye on the dough to see that it had risen enough to put in the oven.

The baking is done year round, although during the winter it can be done every two weeks, since the bread can be kept cool and thus lasts longer than during the summer. The average size of a batch varies from fifteen to twenty-four loaves; it all depends on the number of mouths to feed. The morning is spent preparing the dough, and the bread is baked in the afternoon. Often, when the mother was pregnant or when the winter was too cold, this lengthy preparation was the responsibility of the father. Many wives were very proud of their husbands' talent for kneading the dough. Because of their physical strength, some men were even more skilful than the women at softening the dough and making it rise.[62]

Preparing the Oven

As mentioned above, when the dough is rising for the last time a fire is laid in the oven. This task is almost a ritual and is performed in a festive atmosphere, with the whole family participating.

The oven is heated with special wood that is cut to fit the length of the hearth to ensure an even distribution of heat. It is dry wood, cut very thin. Cedar is the first choice because it burns quickly; failing this, dry pine, spruce, good branches of balsam fir, aspen, driftwood, small logs, or whatever is available is used. This wood is always stacked near the oven, and no one is allowed to touch it. About fifteen pieces are usually required for a good fire, and two fires are the general rule. The wood is crisscrossed over the whole surface of the hearth. For the first fire, it might be placed near the doors and then pushed to the back of the oven to make room for the second fire.[63] The wood is laid out to form a cage or lattice, or it may be positioned like a pyramid or tent. These various ways of laying the fire provide better air circulation, and make the fire draw well. Small pieces of dried bark are placed between the logs.

The mother, father, or eldest child lights the bark that gradually spreads the fire through the wood. The doors are left wide open for ventilation. The flame plays along the walls of the dome and heats them, while heating the hearth at the same time. The fire cracks, hisses, and spreads from one piece of wood to the next[64] as the oven roars and belches black smoke. The wood crackles and finally settles into mounds of burning embers, which are left to cool down.

A fire rake is used to spread out the embers on the hearth. The doors and air holes are closed to allow the heat to penetrate into the walls and recesses of the oven. If the oven is equipped with a small opening at the rear, this is stopped up with a wooden plug. The heating process lasts about an hour and a half. A special tool is used to remove the embers from the oven, and they are then thrown into an old bucket and extinguished. Sometimes the embers are spread out at the sides, the back, or the front of the oven, if the correct temperature has not been attained. Sometimes they are left in the oven during the baking.[65]

A variety of tried and tested methods are used to determine whether the oven has reached the right temperature. The most common is to extend the hand and forearm into the oven while counting up to a certain number, which varies from person to person—4, 10, 20, 25, or 32.[66] Each housewife has her own point of reference. If she is able to keep her arm in the oven until she reaches her number, the oven is ready. On the other hand, if she has to withdraw her arm before this, the oven is still too hot and is allowed a further period of cooling by opening the doors for a few minutes. Another test is to place a piece of newspaper in the oven and see how quickly it catches fire.[67] When the dome is white and the embers have cooled down to ash, the oven is at the correct temperature.

There are other ways to determine the correct temperature. If a handful of pig feed thrown on the hearth takes a while to burn, it is a sign that the moment has arrived.[68] Another way is to check both the dome and the hearth at the same time. It is possible that only the dome is ready and not the hearth. The dome must be an even white in colour. If a handful of flour is thrown on the hearth and turns golden yellow, it is a sign that it is time to put in the bread.[69]

The cook then carefully cleans out the oven and sweeps up the ashes before sending off the whole household, including the children, to bring the pans of puffed-up dough—a real procession![70] While hurrying to complete this task, they must be very careful to avoid shaking up the pans, dropping them, or touching the loaves, in case the dough falls.

Placing the Bread in the Oven

The person doing this task skilfully takes the largest loaves first and lays them side by side at the back and along the sides of the oven, taking care to leave room in the middle and near the front for the loaves cooked directly on the hearth, as well as for the children's loaves, which take less

Checking the temperature of the oven
Blanchette Collection,
NMC AC-21-73-3

Industrious hands and the heat of the
oven walls ensure a successful batch
Public Archives of Canada,
no. PA-44086

time to cook than the large double loaves or the round loaves. Although the task of placing the loaves in the oven is relatively easy, skill is needed in handling the implements used.

Among these implements is the fire rake, which is a long-handled wooden scraper, three inches (7.6 cm) wide. It is used for stoking the fire, spreading out the embers in the oven, and removing the ashes. It is also used occasionally for pulling the bread pans forward before taking them out of the oven.[71] The poker is a long wooden or iron pole for poking the fire and stirring up the embers.[72] The hook, an iron bar with a hook at one end, is used for latching on to the edge of the pans to remove them from the oven.[73] Finally, there is the famous baker's peel. This is a long-handled flat spatula made of light wood. Slipped under the bread pans, it is used for placing the loaves in the oven and for removing them.[74] These implements are usually stored on top of the oven. The baker must be able to handle them with skill despite their awkward length.

The action of placing the loaves in the oven can be imagined as a procession of white shapes disappearing one after the other into a fiery furnace. This scene is accompanied by the rapid movement of the arms; the oven must not be allowed to cool down or the dough will fall. The first bread pan is placed on the baker's peel and carefully lowered to hearth level; it is then inserted in the oven and slid to the back, and a quick flick of the wrist slides it off the peel. The same care is taken with each pan of bread. As soon as the double loaves and the round loaves are in place, the centre and front of the oven are filled with the bread to be cooked directly on the hearth as well as the smaller loaves.

The expression "baking on the hearth" means that the dough is placed directly on the oven floor. Baking in this manner used to be fairly common, and even in more recent times some women continued to use this method when they ran out of baking sheets or when they were unable to find all the pans, which were frequently used for other tasks once the baking was completed. The following description was given by Louis Hémon in *Maria Chapdelaine:*

> On the eve of a baking, Télesphore was sent to hunt up the bread pans, which invariably found their way into all the corners of the house and shed, being in use daily to measure oats for the horse or corn for the fowl, not to mention twenty other casual purposes they continually served.[75]

Large, deep containers of black-iron plate or tin were generally used for the double loaves, and circular containers for the round loaves. Baking was not done exclusively in pans, according to some of our informants and to various authors who recall the custom of baking on the hearth. One informant in his nineties remembered having seen his maternal grandmother baking bread on the hearth without any container.[76] In 1888, Jean-Baptiste Cloutier described the last stages in the preparation of the loaves, which were simply shaped into balls, sprinkled with flour, and left to rise in a type of trough until the baking. He adds: "Tin pans would also be used to bake the loaves",[77] and further on he describes how the loaves are put into the oven:

The loaves turn golden-brown in the
heat of the oven
Blanchette Collection,
NMC 74-14568

The aroma of freshly baked bread
sharpens the appetite
Marius Barbeau Collection, 1936,
NMC 81100

Each loaf is then placed on a spatula dusted with coarse flour and placed in the oven. . . . The loaves slide off the peel easily, with a slight flick of the wrist. Loaves placed in baking pans do not need this precaution.[78]

This method of baking on the hearth was a favourite for a long time. It was often used when, at the last minute, no pans could be found. To bake in this manner, a thicker, firmer dough is required, or else each loaf should be worked into a longer shape.

I myself have baked on the hearth. The dough is the same as it is for the bread pans. We used to bake the bread on the hearth when we didn't have enough pans. I kneaded my bread in the same way and left it to rise on a little board, but I shaped longer and narrower loaves. When it was time to do the baking, I carried my little board—with the bread on it—to the oven as soon as the pans containing the other loaves had been placed at the back of the oven. I swept out the opening of the oven and made sure that the hearth was clean. Then I took a loaf and squeezed it in the middle until it was almost separated into two parts. I folded one part over the other after placing it on the peel. I hit it lightly with my fist to make the two parts stick together and placed it on the hearth, using the peel and my other hand. That is all there was to it.[79]

When all the loaves are properly positioned in the oven, the children's round loaves are lined up at the door. They are put there because they are small and do not require much baking—half to three-quarters of an hour, approximately.

The doors of the oven are then closed. If the oven is too hot and the heat forms the crust too quickly, there is a danger that the bread will not rise properly and that the crust will burn. This is avoided by leaving the air holes or the door open for ventilation.[80] The bread is in the oven for an average of an hour and a half.[81] Loaves cooked in pans rise higher than those baked on the hearth, but eventually they all turn brown and puff up. The heat sets the bread, and the silence of the oven is broken only by the sound of air bubbles escaping from the dough. As she waits patiently, the cook spends the last few minutes imagining a beautiful batch of golden-brown well-shaped loaves.[82]

When the cooking time is up, she checks the colour, takes a loaf in her hands and strikes the bottom of the crust; if it makes a hollow sound, it is a sign that the baking is finished.[83]

Removing the Bread from the Oven

Everyone is on hand for the magic moment when the loaves are taken out of the oven. The aroma of freshly baked bread sharpens the appetite. With the bread hook, the pans are slid onto the peel. One by one they are removed from the pans and set on a table near the oven. To prevent the bread from falling, the loaves are carefully laid down on their sides[84] to cool[85] and dry out.[86] Some people arrange them standing on end in rows, to let them settle.[87] Others let them dry for a few minutes in the pans and then turn them over to rest on the top crust.[88] Still others lay them out side by side in closely packed rows.

The place where the bread is kept and the containers used to keep it fresh vary from region to region. The dough box is certainly an ideal place,[89] but sometimes bread is kept in cupboards in the oven shed,[90] in the cellar,[91] in the kitchen, or in the dairy shed during the summer months.[92] Milk churns are airtight and thus keep the bread soft.[93] Apple barrels might also be used.[94] Once the oven has cooled down, it is another good place to store the bread.[95] Among some of the older people accustomed to frugal living, we heard about the practice of stringing the loaves on a skewer and drying them in the attic, thus reducing the amount eaten by the children. This practice was rather rare, however, though in some families bread was distributed only once during a meal.

Types of Bread

Country people call the staple food prepared at home in their ovens *pain de ménage*, which means "household bread", or *pain de famille*, which means "family bread"; the terms indicate their disapproval of bakery bread.

Homemade bread has numerous other names, depending on its shape and sometimes on its composition. There are, for example, double loaves (two rounds of dough pressed together), single round loaves, braided loaves, bread in the shape of a mushroom, and long loaves, not to mention *gâteau d'habitant* ("farmer's cake"), which is similar to ordinary bread but sweeter.

All the different types of bread—white, whole-wheat, bran, rye, barley, buckwheat, and aniseed-flavoured—are cooked in the same fashion.

Consumption

The large consumption of bread in Quebec families was always accompanied by a feeling of great respect. Because bread had a sacred quality about it, its distribution was surrounded by certain rituals that were scrupulously followed by the father or grandfather at the table.

The loaf of bread was placed on the table near the plate of the head of the family. Before cutting the first slice, he would give thanks to God by tracing a cross on the end of the loaf with the knife. He would then wipe the blade of the knife on the hem of his shirt, cut the bread, and distribute slices to those present, starting with oldest person at the table and ending with the youngest child. Our informants had the following comments: "While he was alive my grandfather cut the bread; before slicing it he traced a cross on it with his knife. Bread is given out to those present in order of status, starting with the oldest."[96] "The head of the household made a sign of the cross over the bread before cutting it."[97] "The father serves the bread and makes a cross on it before slicing it to

The bread oven was life itself
Marius Barbeau Collection,
NMC 81099

In a language rich in metaphor, children
are often referred to as loaves of bread
Blanchette Collection,
NMC AC-21-74-4

ensure that there will always be bread on the table. He serves the eldest first and the youngest last."[98] With very few exceptions, this custom disappeared as it became easier to obtain bread: "Today bread is easy to obtain, but at that time people had respect for it."[99]

Descriptions of these everyday rituals may be found in French-Canadian literature. Among others, Albert Laberge writes in *La Scouine*:

With his black-handled pointed knife, Urgèle Deschamps, who was sitting at the head of the table, quickly drew a cross on the loaf that his wife, Mâço, had just taken out of the dough box. After making the sign of Redemption over the supper bread, he then began cutting slices and piling them in front of him.[100]

The custom of breaking bread does not seem to have existed. It was considered highly improper and a grave insult to the head of the house.[101]

While successful batches adorned the table, there were many different uses for those that were not successful. Loaves that were heavy or chewy were used as feed for poultry and pigs.[102] Dry bread was used for making pudding.[103] The crust of burnt bread was used in the preparation of a type of coffee greatly enjoyed by rural people: "With the crust of burnt bread, we made coffee with hot milk. This was a real treat."[104] Burnt crumbs were soaked in boiling water or mixed with roasted barley: "Roasted barley was added to the burnt breadcrumbs. Roasted barley is ground up with the burnt breadcrumbs to make a coffee-like beverage."[105] In the Lower St. Lawrence and the Gaspé regions, wine is made with the crust of burnt bread. One of our informants told us the following:

Old people used to make wine with the crusts of burnt bread, raisins, oranges, yeast, and sugar. They left it to ferment for three weeks to a month in a pot covered with a cloth until it was ready to drink. It was something like porter. Women used to drink it for energy.[106]

Another added:

Burnt bread would be used for making coffee, and some would make porter by adding hops, yeast, molasses, sugar, and water.[107]

Burnt crusts were also used to cure diarrhoea among the animals.[108]

Some of the common home remedies in the Gaspé region were based on the supposed medicinal properties of bread. It was recommended, for example, to drink an infusion made with bread crusts to speed up the delivery of a baby.[109] To soothe an insect bite, one was advised to "apply a poultice made of bread dough, molasses, and butter."[110]

Chapter IV

The Oral Tradition

Popular Sayings and Expressions

The bread oven, together with all the various activities related to it, is an important and respected aspect of Quebec tradition, and has given rise to a multitude of wise and witty popular sayings and expressions that have social or moral implications. The rural people of Quebec have a vivid expression to fit almost every situation.

On the whole, most references to the oven are closely connected with life itself: "We were brought up in the shadow of the oven."[1] "The oven is life itself."[2] The mother's role of ensuring the continuity of the life cycle is also attributed to the bread oven.[3]

On occasion, the feelings of frustration and impatience brought on by continued contact with other people are expressed in the phrase "to toss someone under the oven",[4] meaning to send someone packing. This refers to the common practice of throwing away underneath the oven dangerous pieces of glass and other useless or harmful trash. The expression "to heat the oven" is used to mean "to drink alcohol".[5] Someone who has a dirty face may be accused of "bearing traces of the oven latch on his face".[6] The failure of some undertaking may be expressed by saying that it is "as successful as an empty oven".[7]

The parts of the oven and the baking tools are also used in figurative speech. Thus, it might be said that a small opening is "no bigger than the mouth of the oven".[8] When one person ridicules another while behaving no better himself, he is like "the baker's peel making fun of the fire rake".[9] The dough box is used as a measure of comparison, as when a small child is said to be "as tall as the dough box".[10] In other circumstances, the dough box and bread-bin are closely associated with childbearing and children in general. In large families, there is no need to worry about the future because "when the good Lord fills the cradle, He doesn't forget to fill the bread-bin".[11] Children are said to ensure the continuity of the family in the same way that bread ensures its survival. Children are often compared to loaves of bread; each child born to a family becomes "one more loaf in the bread-bin",[12] and when misfortune strikes and takes the life of a child it is said that the mother "loses a loaf from her batch".[13] A mother will often boast about her children by saying that they are "as good as good bread".[14] In some areas, the youngest children are compared to the "crumbs in the bottom of the bread-bin",[15] and a child who is growing very quickly "is rising like dough in the dough box".[16] Comparisons are also made in other contexts. For example, when the larder is empty and there is almost nothing left to eat, it is time to "eat

the crumbs in the bottom of the bread-bin".[17] The expression "to be a crumb" is used for a person who is stingy. When someone is in trouble or is in an awkward situation, he will complain of "being in the dough box".[18]

Because of its importance, shape and texture, bread is the source of numerous popular sayings and expressions. "Did you bake?"[19] This is a typical rural way of asking for bread at the table. A begger is said to "ask for his bread".[20] A person who is wealthy is described as having his bread already baked.[21] An egoist or a miser "eats his bread from his pocket or from his bag".[22] A lazy person "is not worth the bread he eats".[23] When someone has a lot of work to do, he may say that he has "bread on his board".[24] To deny oneself for another's benefit is frequently expressed as "taking bread out of one's mouth".[25] A person boasting that he paid a very low price for an object would say that he acquired it for "a piece of bread".[26]

Unannounced visitors arriving at the home of a stingy person at mealtime might say jokingly at the door, "Hide the bread."[27] A very kind person would be described as being "as good as good bread".[28] Somebody with a long, sad face would be asked if he had "lost a loaf from his batch".[29] One who believes that he will never be successful repeatedly uses this phrase in conversation: "When you are born for small loaves, what's the use. . . ."[30] To "earn one's bread by the sweat of one's brow" indicates the hard work necessary to support a family.[31] A temporary period of misfortune or poverty is accepted by saying, "If there's no bread, we'll just have to eat the leaven."[32] The belief that obstacles and difficulties in life allow a keener appreciation of the success and happines that is bound to follow is expressed by: "In life one always has to start by eating black bread before eating the white."[33] Here black bread is synonymous with poverty, while white bread symbolizes affluence.

There is something sacred about bread, and in most families waste is not tolerated: "Waste not the bread of the Lord."[34] Bread is also related to other areas of family life. When husbands continue to remain courteous and attentive to their wives, it is said that "the wedding bread is still fresh."[35] Similarly, at the engagement of a son, before giving his final approval, the father will "test the daughter-in-law",[36] which means that he will sample the bread she makes and assess her competence in other household skills as well. A woman who cooks poorly is "a woman of heavy bread".[37]

A person's character is also described in terms of bread. A rude, insensitive, or ill-mannered person is said to be "coarse as barley bread".[38] A good-for-nothing, inept, or clumsy person might be called "suet bread".[39] An unpleasant neighbour could be nicknamed "gingerbread".[40]

The batch of loaves as a unit has also left its mark on the language. For example, a cook remarking on the poor quality of the loaves as they come out of the oven might exclaim regretfully over her "batch of potash".[41]

Regarding flour, one might hear: "The devil shat in my flour";[42] this expression is used especially when the weed vetch has been milled with the wheat, thus giving it a bitter taste. The saying "the devil's flour

"This old oven saw many harvests and many generations. It must have provided sustenance for a good number of families!" (Bouchard 1917–18)
Public Archives of Canada,
no. PA-43333

turns to bran" is used to mean that "ill-gotten gains never prosper."[43] Zany, exuberant people are sometimes said to be "under the flour",[44] a reference to the whitened faces of circus clowns.

Finally, when the loaves are full of air holes, children will amuse themselves by pretending that they can "play hide-and-seek between the bread and the crust".[45]

Songs

The oven and the batch of loaves have been immortalized in songs. In the old days women hummed lively tunes as they baked. Several of our informants sang parts of the old songs for us, such as *Le petit Grégoire* ("Little Gregory"),[46] *La berceuse blanche* ("The White Cradle Song"),[47] *Les blés d'or* ("Golden Corn"),[48] and *Le bon pain d'habitant* ("Good Country Bread"). In the first song, there is a mocking comparison with the dough box.

> *La maman du petit homme*
> *Lui dit un matin,*
> *À seize ans t'es haut tout comme*
> *Notre huche à pain.**

The second rhyme expresses the feeling of security that comes with having bread in the house:

> *Avez-vous faim?*
> *Tout plein les huches*
> *Y a du pain.***

In a number of these old songs, we again find the devil theme in connection with the oven:

> *Le diable a été su le boulanger,*
> *C'est pour l'affaire qui s'est fait attraper.*
> *Le boulanger l'a pris l'a fourré dans son four*
> *Mais l'diable y a joué un cré bon tour,*
> *Y a parti avec le darrière du four.*[49]***

This version is similar to the one discovered by Marcel Rioux entitled *Le diable est venu dans la ville*[50] ("The Devil Came to Town"). In fact, this song is also known under the title *Le diable bafoué* ("The Devil Scorned"), and is a counterpoint to *La récolte du diable* ("The Devil's Harvest"). This time the tradesmen get together to take their revenge on the devil, who always manages to escape, but only after many adventures.

Other songs, some lighthearted and others more serious, can be added to this list. To name a few, there is *Le vol des pâtés chauds* ("The Theft of the Hot Pies"), in which Michaud lives to regret his greediness. Then there is *Les jours de la semaine* ("The Days of the Week"), in which each day of the week has its particular task: "Wednesday is bread-baking

---

*One morning a mother said to her son: "Now you are sixteen, you're as tall as the dough box."
**If you are hungry, the bins are full of bread.
***The devil visited the baker, who caught him at his mischief and stuffed him in the oven. But the devil had the last laugh—he left, taking the back of the oven with him.

day."[51] The verses of the song entitled *Le pain* ("Bread") sing the praises of the staff of life. The refrain is as follows:

> *Le pain, le pain*
> *Est du genre humain*
> *Le mets le plus sain.*
> *Vive le pain!*[52]*

Finally, while stoking the oven, the following lively refrain is sung: "Split the wood, heat the oven."[53]

People no longer give rhythm to their work by singing as they go about various tasks. Our informants assured us that in the old days people always sang as they worked. It seems that the songs disappeared as the bread ovens fell into disuse.

Stories and Legends

Just as it lives on in old songs, the oven also appears in stories and legends, often forming a focus for diabolical manifestations. The oven is used in explanations of such cosmic and existential realities as the origin of life, the challenges faced by man, and man's aspirations.

Here we are concerned mainly with stories in anecdotal form. One of the themes treated is that of punishment. The oven is a place of suffering, no doubt because of its somewhat forbidding appearance: dark and cramped, it contains the fire that punishes and the heat that transforms. "In stories, people who have to be punished or got rid of are shut up in the oven."[54] In some stories, the oven is the place of combat between Saint Peter and Satan, and in others it is the site of challenges between man and the devil.

Beliefs such as these are communicated in a variety of legends. Here are a few anecdotes that our informants drew from their memories:

> It so happened that, on his rounds of the parish, the priest found himself at the house of a poor woman. This woman had two children, a boy and a girl. Because the children were ashamed of their old clothes, they went to hide in the bread oven. During his visit the priest asked the woman where her children were . . . (silence). As he was leaving he passed in front of the bread oven; the doors opened and two little demons came out.[55]

The old lady who told us this story said that it was punishment for hiding from the priest. The episode contains certain similarities to the following:

> A mother, wanting to punish her two children, locked them in the oven. She closed the oven and heated it, and when she opened it again two little bears came out, one female and the other male.[56]

Then there is the unfortunate incident connected with a spell that caused a transformation to take place inside the oven:

> There used to be a lot of beggars roaming about. When the women were alone with their children they were often afraid. One

*Bread is the healthiest food to eat. Long live bread!

time, a woman hid her child in the oven to protect him. When the beggar was gone, she went to get her child and found a monkey in his place.[57]

Though our collection of stories and legends is small, we can see a recurring theme—the oven is shown as a place of punishment and of transformation. The oven is a mediator. All that is undesirable in life is put in the bread oven, where metamorphosis will occur.

Popular Beliefs, Spells, Incantations, and Omens

The dread of unknown forces, nourished by ignorance, created a variety of beliefs, including many connected with the making of bread and its use. Both the literature and the memories of our informants reveal the obsessions of the popular imagination.

The belief that beggars were able to cast evil spells was the most common myth, and we found it in one village after another. Beggars were reputed to have great powers: "They were either a blessing or a curse."[58] If they were treated with impatience or were refused alms, food, or shelter, they would call down all manner of curses and evil fortune on the family. Any failure or anything that went wrong thereafter was believed to be the result of the beggar's evil powers.

One wonders how many women with their hands in the bread dough received curses of this type and were not able to bake for years afterwards! There were many such cases, but we will mention only a few of the most interesting ones, omitting the names of our informants. At lac Saint-Jean we were told the following:

> One day my mother was kneading her bread, and since she had her hands in the dough she refused to give money to a beggar. The bread did not rise, and from that day on all of her batches failed and she never again made a successful batch of loaves. She was sure that the beggar had placed a spell on her.

In Charlevoix we were told:

> When the women failed in their bread making or when the bread was sour or smelled rotten, they were all too willing to believe that it was a spell placed on them by a beggar to whom they had not given alms.

On Île d'Orléans we were told: "If women made poor batches several times in a row, they said that someone had cast a spell on them." If the bread did not last more than a couple of days, if it was too doughy or became mouldy, or if successive batches failed, the beggars were usually blamed.[59]

Was it necessary to put up with these misfortunes? Was there any way to cast them off? By closely following certain rites it was possible to remove the evil spells from the bread. Some of these involved the use of fire and needles, or a wedding band. For example, needles would be poked into a loaf from the failed batch, and it would then be thrown into the fire to burn. It was believed that the person who cast the spell would suffer the punishment endured by the bread, and would then remove the spell to end

The "fruits of the oven" are laid carefully on end so that they will retain their shape while cooling
Public Archives of Canada,
no. PA-44083

"We were brought up in the shadow of the oven."
Les chemins de fer nationaux, Almanach de l'Action sociale catholique, 1929

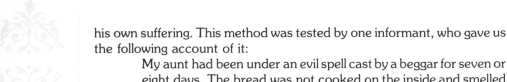

his own suffering. This method was tested by one informant, who gave us the following account of it:

> My aunt had been under an evil spell cast by a beggar for seven or eight days. The bread was not cooked on the inside and smelled like rotten meat, although the crust was the way it should be. The old folks used to say that poking needles into the bread and burning it would cast off a spell. So I did that, and the next day my aunt made some bread and it was as successful as it had been before the spell.[60]

Another way to counteract the spell would be for the woman to place her wedding band in the new dough.[61]

Pierre-Georges Roy points out that "beggars in former times had the reputation of casting evil spells. . . . If an animal died in a strange manner, if the bread burned in the fire, if the laying hens had very few chicks, or if a batch of soap was a failure, the blame was always laid on an evil spell."[62] Today, bakers no longer complain of evil spells, but, as another informant pointed out, "Nowadays with the new welfare laws you don't see beggars any more."

In addition to the importance given to spells, the physical condition of the woman doing the baking might affect the success of the bread. Thus, if a woman who has a fever bakes bread, the dough will not rise.[63] A woman with acidity in her blood will never succeed in making good bread.[64]

We also found other beliefs and customs concerning food. People used to make the sign of the cross over a loaf before slicing it, or they would cross themselves before kneading the dough. This is still a custom in some families and is done to give thanks to God. It is also a way of seeking God's bounty for the days to come: "Always make the sign of the cross over the bread so as to have some the next day."[65] Moreover, certain things must not be done: "If you have to leave the loaf for a minute when you are in the middle of cutting a slice of bread, you must not leave the knife in the bread or bad luck will come to you."[66] For good luck, care is taken to keep blessed bread in an appropriate place. For example, "Blessed bread in the purse will ensure that you always have money."[67] It was also supposed to be easy to find the body of a drowned person with the help of a piece of blessed bread: "Throw a piece of blessed bread in the water. It will float and then begin to spin when it is above the spot where the body is lying."[68]

The ill effects of certain natural phenomena were also cause for concern. For example, thunderstorms were feared because the leaven would break up and the dough would not rise.[69]

Conclusions

From the techniques of oven building, we progressed to the main purpose for which they are built—baking bread. We concluded by exploring the significance of these two activities as revealed in the oral tradition.

We included a few historical references in order to provide a time frame for the phenomena encountered during our research and fieldwork. The bread oven is shown to be fundamentally connected to economic self-sufficiency, being very useful in pre-industrial regions and even in the rural areas of an industrialized country. Unfavourable socio-economic conditions can precipitate a return to the methods of self-sufficiency.

We did not limit this study to mere technical description because we believed that, in order to fully comprehend any object forming part of the material culture, it is important to consider how it was viewed in the oral tradition.

This approach enabled us to make two general observations: firstly, the *habitant* has an intimate knowledge of the properties of the materials he uses, and he expresses his knowledge with a particularly vivid vocabulary; secondly, the function of the bread oven is one of transformation, and its power to do this is reflected in the oral tradition surrounding it.

Let us take a brief look at the basis for these statements. In the language he uses, the farmer constantly refers to familiar phenomena for purposes of comparison and analogy. Let us look, for example, at the rich vocabulary used to describe clay ovens. The farmer readily compares the various stages in the construction of the clay oven to the preparation of

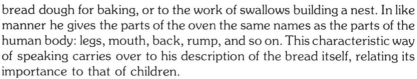

bread dough for baking, or to the work of swallows building a nest. In like manner he gives the parts of the oven the same names as the parts of the human body: legs, mouth, back, rump, and so on. This characteristic way of speaking carries over to his description of the bread itself, relating its importance to that of children.

We must point out that, because ovens have fallen into disuse, the source of a rich imagery has dried up, with the result that it was very difficult to gather the few fragments we did manage to collect. On the other hand, it was easier to compile expressions concerning bread itself simply because the baking of bread in the home has survived, and the vocabulary has thus been maintained.

As for the transformation that takes place in the oven, it results from the ability of the oven walls to retain the necessary heat. The oven converts into delicious bread a raw dough that itself is considered inedible. It also changes vegetable matter that must first be dried to be usable. It kills the germs that infest the clothing of the sick. This capacity for material transformation is reflected in the oral tradition. In tales and legends, all that is undesirable in life, everything unpleasant, undergoes a metamorphosis in the oven.

In conclusion, it is clear that the role of the bread oven in daily life, language, and legend reveals its dynamic relationship with those who make it and those who use it.

Notes

The abbreviation Inf. stands for infor-
mant(s). Each informant has been
assigned a field number (see the list on
page 112). The abbreviation AJM
stands for Archives judiciaires de
Montréal (Montreal Judicial Archives);
AJQ stands for Archives judiciaires de
Québec (Quebec City Judicial
Archives).

Notes on the Introduction

1 Anderson 1970: 57.
2 Séguin 1967, 1969.
3 Savard 1943: 143–46.
4 Bouchard 1917–18; 1926: 78–83.
5 Diderot and d'Alembert 1782: 151–54.
6 Ibid.: 152.
7 Labignette 1964: 497: Pierre-Georges
  Roy 1924: 257–59.
8 The documents studied were provided
  by Dr. Robert-Lionel Séguin, director of
  the Centre de documentation en
  civilisation traditionnelle, Université
  du Québec à Trois-Rivières, and by
  Mr. Fernand Caron of the Centre de
  documentation de la Place Royale,
  Ministère des Affaires culturelles in
  Quebec City. The records analysed are
  from the Montreal Judicial Archives:
  Anthoine Adhémar (1668–1714),
  Jean-Baptiste Adhémar (1714–54), and

Bénigne Basset (1657–99); and from the
Quebec City Judicial Archives:
Guillaume Audouart (1647–63), Louis
Chambalon (1692–1716), Pierre Duquet
(1663–87), Michel Fillion (1660–88),
François Genaple (1682–1709), and
Gilles Rageot (1666–92).
9 Many of the notarial documents are
  missing from the archives. According to
  André Vachon (1962), the minutes of
  notaries were not conserved with great
  care before 1733.

Notes on Chapter I

1 Inf. 32, 121.
2 The dome is outside but the oven doors
  open inside, under cover.
3 Inf. 188.
4 Inf. 18, 44, 73, 78, 86, 88, 89, 95, 102,
  107, 113, 127, 144, 165, 169, 177, 192,
  193, 200, 209, 214.
5 Inf. 31, 34, 53, 61, 82, 90, 101, 103, 110,
  112, 125, 126, 139.
6 Inf. 64, 171, 172.
7 Inf. 175.
8 Inf. 57, 118.
9 Inf. 55, 86.
10 Inf. 175.
11 Inf. 106.
12 Inf. 59, 60, 119.
13 Inf. 59.

14 Inf. 61, 80.
15 Inf. 86.
16 Inf. 78.
17 Inf. 101, 103.
18 Inf. 139.
19 Inf. 166.
20 Inf. 53.
21 Inf. 62, 192, 200, 201.
22 Inf. 103.
23 Inf. 118, 125.
24 Inf. 118.
25 Inf. 126.
26 Inf. 92, 110.
27 Inf. 214.
28 Inf. 61, 80, 92.
29 Inf. 41, 46, 73, 86, 99, 102, 111, 117, 120.
30 Inf. 125, 145.
31 Inf. 18, 33, 62, 64, 86, 88, 89, 96, 106, 110, 116, 135, 139, 172, 178, 200.
32 Mr. René Desruisseaux, 14 July 1972: personal communication. He worked at the Bernier foundry, Lotbinière.
33 Ibid.
34 Marcel Moussette, 29 Nov. 1972: personal communication. He gave us the following information:
    Bernier Foundry:
    Opened around 1852 in Lotbinière. Henri Bernier was in partnership with E.E. Méthot until 1854.
    The foundry was in operation until 1925.
    Méthot Foundry:
    E.E. Méthot probably opened his own foundry towards the end of the 1850s (1859).
    In 1868 the foundry was purchased by J.L.O. Vidal.
    The foundry was sold by auction in 1874."
35 Ibid.
36 Inf. 95, 172.
37 Bouchard 1917–18: 408.
38 Inf. 110.
39 Inf. 1, 27, 30.
40 Inf. 214.
41 Inf. 41, 56, 84, 103, 108, 113, 165, 169, 170, 171, 172, 177, 178, 201, 214; Bouchard 1917–18: 407.
42 Inf. 30, 33, 44, 46, 53, 58, 59, 60, 88, 89, 144.
43 Inf. 106, 118, 175, 176.
44 Inf. 108, 175.
45 Inf. 37, 185, 190.
46 Inf. 121.
47 Inf. 125.
48 Inf. 116, 124, 135, 162, 180.
49 Inf. 190, 207.
50 Inf. 62.
51 Inf. 103.
52 Inf. 177.
53 Inf. 106.
54 Inf. 86.
55 Inf. 106.
56 Inf. 41, 117, 166.
57 Inf. 91, 165.
58 Inf. 108, 170.
59 Inf. 95, 99, 113, 134, 193.
60 Inf. 18, 33, 80, 90, 133, 201.
61 Inf. 81, 126, 144.
62 Inf. 60.
63 Diderot and d'Alembert 1782: See *Four* ("oven").
64 Inf. 91.
65 Inf. 210, 211, 212, 213.
66 Inf. 46, 57.
67 Inf. 145.
68 Inf. 194.
69 Inf. 159, 210.
70 Inf. 49, 162.
71 Inf. 121.
72 Inf. 188.
73 Paré 1940: 18.
74 Inf. 105, 119, 120, 159, 160, 161, 194, 197, 203, 208, 210, 212, 213.
75 Inf. 120, 195, 203.
76 Inf. 194.
77 Bénigne Basset, AJM, 17 July 1667: Record of the verbal appraisal of the property belonging to the late Jean Cicot.
78 Michel Fillion, AJQ, 27 Mar. 1677: Farming lease by Jean Millois to Jacques Parent.
79 Anthoine Adhémar, AJM, 5 Feb. 1699: Sale by Mr. le Gardeur and Dame de St. pere, his wife, to Mr. Amyault; 11 Apr. 1699: "Inventory of the property of the deceased Le Cour, Bouchard, and Le Blanc, his wife.
80 Inf. 23, 104, 122, 123, 138, 141, 142, 147, 148, 152, 153, 157, 168, 182, 183, 184, 186, 187, 188, 189, 190, 196, 204, 205.
81 Inf. 205.
82 Inf. 104, 122, 123, 142, 148, 153, 182, 183, 186, 187, 188, 189, 191, 196, 204.
83 Inf. 141.
84 Inf. 91, 168.
85 Inf. 32, 123, 138, 141, 148, 152, 168, 182, 184, 186, 187.
86 Inf. 155, 157, 189.
87 Inf. 189.
88 Inf. 33, 94.
89 Inf. 18, 25, 26, 32, 33, 37, 42, 47, 54, 55, 58, 59, 63, 74, 78, 80, 82, 117, 152, 159, 163, 170, 192, 201.
90 Inf. 3, 46, 60, 71, 86, 91, 92, 96, 107, 108, 126, 153, 165, 168, 169, 171, 189, 193, 194, 206.
91 Inf. 56, 71, 77, 103, 125.
92 In *La Corvée*, second literary competition of the Société Saint-Jean-Baptiste de Montréal, 1917, p. 119.
93 Inf. 144.
94 Inf. 193.
95 *La Corvée*, op. cit., p. 122.
96 Inf. 48, 93, 108.
97 Inf. 153.
98 Inf. 96, 100, 214.

99   Inf. 28, 32, 73, 84, 91, 145, 179.
100 Inf. 156.
101 Inf. 81, 107.
102 See Introduction, note 8.
103 François Genaple, AJQ, 14 Apr. 1704: Farming lease by Pre LeClerc to Jacques Gervais.
104 François Genaple, AJQ, 10 Mar. 1709: Lease by the Widow Minet to Jean Cornuau.
105 Bénigne Basset, AJM, 3 July 1673: Inventory of the personal estate and property of the late Anthoine Courtemanche, called Jollycoeur.
106 Louis Chambalon, AJQ, 11 May 1692: Contract between Louis Prat and André Coutron on behalf of Louis Jolliet.
107 Anthoine Adhémar, AJM, 2 May 1699: Rental lease by Decarry to Delaunay.
108 Séguin 1967: 188.
109 The value of the minot changed with time, and it is difficult to compare it with modern systems of measurement. Four minots, however, equal one setier (Séguin 1967: 188; Trudel 1968: 238). One setier equals 150 to 300 litres (*Petit Robert* dictionary).
110 François Genaple, AJQ, 14 Aug. 1700: Sale of house and property by S. Denis Mallet to Jq. Pajan.
111 Anthoine Adhémar, AJM, 4 May 1698: Rental lease by de Veaux and his spouse to Bourbon.
112 Jean-Baptiste Adhémar, AJM, 26 Jan. 1727: Estimate and contract made between Mr. Lapalme and Vincent Rorant.
113 Two-thirds of the outdoor ovens observed were made of clay and one-third were made of brick.
114 Kniffen (1960) explained that, in French Louisiana, the presence or absence of outdoor bread ovens depended upon the availability of wheat. In fact, wheat seems to have been the only grain used for baking bread in the outdoor French ovens in that region. Later in this study, we will see that other grains in addition to wheat were used for baking bread in French Canada.
115 Glassie 1968: 8 ff.
116 Inf. 1, 2, 92, 103.
117 Carmen Roy 1962: 185.
118 Inf. 1, 169.
119 Inf. 160.
120 Jean-Claude Dupont, 23 Oct. 1972: personal communication.
121 Savard 1943: 146.
122 Inf. 92, 166, 214.
123 Inf. 97.
124 Inf. 126.
125 Inf. 82.
126 Barbeau 1942: 204; Inf. 62.
127 Inf. 34, 36.

128 Inf. 101, 109.
129 Girard 1967: 17.
130 Lavoie 1971: 51.

Notes on Chapter II

1 River named after Mars Simard, the first settler at the mouth of the river in 1838 (Tremblay 1968: 239).
2 Valin 1947: 314.
3 Savard 1943: 146.
4 Ibid.

Notes on Chapter III

1 Bergeron 1947: 124.
2 Inf. 56.
3 Nadeau 1916.
4 Paré 1940.
5 Ibid.: 30.
6 Paré 1934: back cover.
7 Labignette 1964: 490.
8 Hamelin 1960: 66.
9 Labrie 1970: 3.
10 Fauteux 1927: 351, 360.
11 Liger 1732 (Vol. 1): 80.
12 Lefebvre 1961: 103.
13 Berthelot 1924: 104.
14 Russell 1857: 125–26.
15 Nadeau 1916: 13.
16 Paré 1940: 1.
17 Nadeau 1916.
18 Jean-Charles Magnan, 2 Dec. 1972: personal communication.
19 Inf. 103.
20 Inf. 92, 96, 126, 166.
21 Inf. 104, 182.
22 Cloutier 1888: 112.
23 Inf. 36, 133.
24 Falardeau, Garigue, and Gérin 1968: 93.
25 Inf. 91.
26 Rousseau 1938: 12.
27 Paré 1940: 6.
28 Liger 1732 (Vol. 1): 83–84.
29 Rousseau 1938: 12.
30 Inf. 56, 81, 86, 93, 96, 101, 103, 108, 109, 125, 126, 133, 166, 171, 173, 189, 194, 201, 207, 215.
31 Cloutier 1888: 113.
32 Paré 1940: 7.
33 Rousseau 1938: 12.
34 Inf. 189.
35 Inf. 149.
36 Inf. 34, 41, 149.
37 Inf. 41, 54, 173.
38 Inf. 215.
39 Inf. 25, 43, 104, 151.
40 Inf. 18, 34, 41, 54, 58, 92, 149, 173, 182, 189, 207.
41 Inf. 193.
42 Inf. 34, 96, 166.
43 Inf. 206.

44 Inf. 107, 133.
45 Nadeau 1916: 16.
46 Ibid.: 14.
47 Paré 1940: 2.
48 Inf. 13.
49 Inf. 42, 84, 173, 205.
50 Inf. 36.
51 Inf. 78.
52 Inf. 215.
53 Inf. 54, 55, 149.
54 Dupont 1971.
55 Ibid.
56 Ibid.
57 Bergeron 1947: 35.
58 Inf. 189.
59 Liger 1732 (Vol. 1): 85.
60 Lily Boily-Pelletier, 4 Dec. 1972: personal communication.
61 Inf. 55, 101.
62 Inf. 126, 153.
63 Inf. 152.
64 Inf. 86.
65 Inf. 18, 53, 170.
66 This depends on the size of the oven and the material it is made of. The higher the number the higher the person's tolerance to heat.
67 Inf. 214.
68 Inf. 188.
69 Inf. 103.
70 Inf. 152.
71 Inf. 46, 51, 62, 68, 86, 92, 117, 153, 160, 169, 174, 193, 201.
72 Inf. 56, 121, 169.
73 Inf. 96, 144.
74 Inf. 54, 55, 78, 166, 193.
75 Hémon 1957: 79.
76 Inf. 188.
77 Cloutier 1888: 114.
78 Ibid.: 114–15.
79 Inf. 193.
80 Inf. 81, 82, 192, 206.
81 Inf. 46, 54, 59, 62, 77, 80, 86, 91, 93, 96, 104, 107, 117, 121, 126, 193, 200.
82 Inf. 121.
83 Inf. 192.
84 Inf. 84, 86, 90, 96, 101, 104, 107, 126, 144, 146, 153, 171.
85 Inf. 121.
86 Inf. 103.
87 Inf. 91, 92, 117, 153.
88 Inf. 103, 152, 166, 169, 182, 201, 206.
89 Inf. 91, 107, 117, 121, 156, 160.
90 Inf. 153.
91 Inf. 152.
92 Inf. 144.
93 Inf. 92, 101.
94 Inf. 96, 206.
95 Inf. 51.
96 Inf. 92.
97 Inf. 214.
98 Inf. 152.
99 Inf. 91.
100 Laberge 1918: 1.

101 Jean-Claude Dupont, Oct. 1972: personal communication.
102 Inf. 107, 146, 159, 175.
103 Inf. 153, 171.
104 Inf. 86.
105 Inf. 189.
106 Inf. 207.
107 Inf. 206.
108 Inf. 214.
109 Carmen Roy 1962: 65.
110 Ibid.: 80.

Notes on Chapter IV

1 Inf. 67.
2 Inf. 32.
3 Our informants communicated very few metaphors or expressions in this regard. However, the reader might refer to Sigmund Freud's interpretation of the oven in his *Introduction to Psychoanalysis*, where the oven is shown as a symbol of woman and the womb. Freud also reports that in some parts of Germany a woman who has just given birth is described as follows: "Her oven has collapsed."
Leslie Abernathy told us that along the Mississippi River in the state of Arkansas, the expression "she has one in the oven" is used to describe a pregnant woman. (Jan. 1973: personal communication)
4 *Glossaire du parler français au Canada*, 1930: 351.
5 Dionne 1909: 334.
6 Ibid.: 333.
7 Ibid.: 334.
8 Inf. 41.
9 Inf. 93.
10 Inf. 51.
11 Lily Boily-Pelletier, 12 Oct. 1972: personal communication.
12 Inf. 25.
13 Inf. 96.
14 Inf. 215.
15 Lacourcière 1950: 76.
16 Dionne 1909: 381.
17 Inf. 51.
18 Inf. 46.
19 Inf. 92.
20 Dionne 1909: 497.
21 Ibid.
22 Bélisle 1957: 875.
23 Ibid.
24 Common meaning.
25 Dionne 1909: 497.
26 Bélisle 1957: 875.
27 Jean-Claude Dupont, Oct. 1972: personal communication.
28 Inf. 215; Lily Boily-Pelletier, Oct. 1972: personal communication.
29 Inf. 56.

30 Édouard Fournier, Victoriaville. Child-
    hood memories, 1952, from the files of
    the Archives de Folklore, université
    Laval.
31 Inf. 215.
32 Inf. 215.
33 Inf. 215.
34 Dupont 1971.
35 Pierre-Georges Roy 1923: 310.
36 Dupont 1971.
37 Ibid.
38 Working papers of Édouard-Zotique
    Massicotte in the manuscripts depart-
    ment, Archives nationales du Québec
    (Quebec Provincial Archives), Montreal.
39 *Glossaire du parler français au
    Canada,* 1930: 489.
40 Jean-Claude Dupont, Oct. 1972: per-
    sonal communication.
41 Inf. 192.
42 Inf. 158.
43 Denise Labelle, 10 Dec. 1952, Archives
    de Folklore, université Laval.
44 *Glossaire du parler français au
    Canada,* 1968: 340.
45 Inf. 200.
46 Inf. 18, 92.
47 Inf. 18.
48 Inf. 92.
49 Inf. 62.
50 Pouinard 1950 (Vol. 2): 62.
51 Allaire 1931: 123.
52 Massicotte, *see* note 38.
53 Gagnon 1908: 112–13.
54 Jean-Claude Dupont, 23 Oct. 1972:
    personal communication.
55 Inf. 164.
56 Dupont 1971.
57 Inf. 121.
58 Inf. 92.
59 More than twenty informants gave us
    details in this regard.
60 Collected in Kamouraska County.
61 Jean-Claude Dupont, Oct. 1972: per-
    sonal communication.
62 Pierre-Georges Roy 1944: 78.
63 Inf. 91.
64 Inf. 96.
65 Carmen Roy 1962: 98; Inf. 152.
66 Carmen Roy 1962: 102.
67 Jacques and Madeleine Rousseau 1950:
    81.
68 Ibid.: 84.
69 Boiteau 1949: 8.

The Informants

1 Mr. and Mrs. Louis-Joseph Simard, Bagotville
2 Mr. Théophile Tremblay, L'Anse-Saint-Jean
3 Mrs. Arthur Boily, Saint-Félicien
4 Mr. Alphonse Badeau, Fortierville
5 Mr. Robert Simard, Chicoutimi
6 Mr. Charles-Albert Desgagné, Saint-Gédéon
7 Mrs. Lily Boily-Pelletier, Montreal
8 Mrs. Ernest Larouche, Saint-Coeur-de-Marie
9 Mr. Louis-Joseph Émond, Port-Alfred
10 Mr. Sylvio Dumas, Quebec
11 Miss Yvonne Fournier, Laterrière
12 Mrs. Adrien Gagné, Laterrière
13 Mr. J.-Adrien Gagnon, Laterrière
14 Mr. J.-Cyrille Émond, Laterrière
15 Mrs. Flavien Grenon, Laterrière
16 Idem
17 Mrs. Elphège Claveau, Bagotville
18 Mr. Louis-Joseph Simard, Bagotville
19 Idem
20 Idem
22 Mr. Jean-Marie Simard, Port-Alfred
23 Miss Madeleine Brassard and Miss Marina Brassard, Chicoutimi-Nord
24 Mrs. Thomas Blanchette, Chicoutimi
25 Mr. and Mrs. Alphonse Blackburn, Chicoutimi
26 Mr. Laurent Beaulieu, Chicoutimi
27 Mrs. Pitt Saulnier, Chicoutimi
28 Mr. Henri Belley, Chicoutimi
29 Mr. Léon Savard, Chicoutimi-Nord
30 Mr. Léonce Villeneuve, Valin
31 Mr. Philippe Lavoie, Saint-Fulgence
32 Mr. Philippe Gagnon, Chicoutimi
33 Mrs. Stella Harvey, Saint-Fulgence
34 Mr. and Mrs. Thomas Harvey, Saint-Fulgence
35 Mrs. François Côté, Valin
36 Mr. and Mrs. Louis-Philippe Turcotte, Saint-Fulgence
37 Mr. François-Xavier Tremblay, Saint-Fulgence
38 Mr. Louis-Joseph Simard, Saint-Fulgence
39 Mr. Napoléon Tremblay, Saint-Fulgence
40 Mr. Edmond Dallaire, Saint-Fulgence
41 Mr. Georges Tremblay called Richard, Saint-Fulgence
42 Mrs. Maurice Morin, Grande-Baie
43 Mr. Marcel Lavoie, Grande-Baie
44 Mr. Edmond Poulin, Grande-Baie
45 Mr. Osias Tremblay, Grande-Baie
46 Mr. Édouard Gagnon, Grande-Baie
47 Mr. Joseph-Noël Claveau, Bagotville
48 Mr. Gérard Gobeil, Chicoutimi
49 Mr. and Mrs. Jean-Charles Tremblay, Chicoutimi
50 Mr. Marcel Lapointe, Chicoutimi
51 Mgr. Victor Tremblay, Chicoutimi
52 Mrs. Monique Bouchard, Jonquière
53 Mrs. Jean-Baptiste Tremblay, Saint-Honoré
54 Mrs. Alias Flaman, Saint-Honoré

55 Mr. Joseph-Hercule Simard, Saint-Ambroise
56 Mr. Johnny Bouchard, Saint-Ambroise
57 Mrs. Jean-Arthur Tremblay, Saint-Ambroise
58 Mrs. Armand Gagné, Saint-Charles-Borromé
59 Mr. Édouard Harvey, Saint-Charles-Borromé
60 Mr. René Gagné, Saint-Charles-Borromé
61 Mr. Paul-Henri Lavoie, Saint-Nazaire
62 Mr. Joseph Gagnon, Saint-Henri-de-Taillon
63 Mr. Joseph Fortin, Sainte-Monique-de-Honfleur
64 Mrs. Charles-Henri St-Pierre, Saint-Augustin
66 Mrs. Lévis Boily, Sainte-Jeanne-d'Arc
67 Mr. Wilfrid Lavoie, Sainte-Jeanne-d'Arc
68 Mrs. Vilemond Néron, Albanel
69 Mr. Serge Audet, Chambord
70 Mr. Joseph Dumais, Lac-Bouchette
71 Mr. René Villeneuve, Chambord
72 Mr. Thomas-Louis Ménard, Chambord
73 Mr. Joseph Ringuette, Chambord-Station
74 Mr. Xavier Duchesne, Saint-Jérôme
76 Mr. Joseph-Albert Lajoie, Notre-Dame-d'Hébertville
77 Mr. Ernest Girard, Notre-Dame-d'Hébertville
78 Mr. Alfred Lessard, Saint-Gédéon
79 Mrs. Jean-Roch Gagnon, Alma
80 Mr. Onésime Laforêt, Hébertville-Station
81 Mr. Édouard Ouellet, Baie-Sainte-Catherine
82 Mr. and Mrs. Joseph Lapointe, Saint-Fidèle
83 Idem
84 Mr. Gonzague Lapointe, Saint-Fidèle
85 Mr. Jacques Lemoïl, Cap-à-l'Aigle
86 Mrs. Edmond Desbiens, Sainte-Mathilde
87 Mr. Dollard Brisson, Cap-à-l'Aigle
88 Mrs. Jean-Paul Tremblay, Cap-à-l'Aigle
89 Mr. David Lapointe, Cap-à-l'Aigle
90 Mr. Antonio Tremblay, Pointe-au-Pic
91 Mr. Xavier Gauthier, Jonquière
92 Mr. Raoul Tremblay, Jonquière
93 Mrs. Ludger Corneau, Jonquière
94 Mrs. Rosaire Cantin, Kénogami
96 Mr. and Mrs. Conrad Boudreault, L'Anse-Saint-Jean
97 Mr. Maurille Lavoie, L'Anse-Saint-Jean
99 Mr. Édouard Lavoie, L'Anse-Saint-Jean
100 Mr. Raoul Bouchard, L'Anse-Saint-Jean
101 Messrs. Edmond Simard and Thomas-Louis Gaudreault, Notre-Dame-des-Monts
102 Mr. Louis-Philippe Tremblay, Sainte-Agnès
103 Mr. Elzéar Bergeron, Saint-Hilarion
104 Mrs. Ferdinand Audette and Mrs. Wilfrid Audette, Saint-Hilarion
105 Mr. Maurice Tremblay, Saint-Urbain
106 Mr. Lucien Bouchard, Baie-Saint-Paul
107 Mrs. Ernest Lajoie, Saint-Urbain
108 Mr. Idola Lavoie, Saint-Urbain
109 Mr. Aimé Boudreault, Saint-Hilarion
110 Mr. Élias Gagnon, Saint-Hilarion
113 Mr. Albert Fortin, Saint-Urbain
114 Mrs. Didime Bolduc, Baie-Saint-Paul
115 Miss Jeanne-d'Arc Simard, Baie-Saint-Paul
116 Mrs. Charles-Eugène Boivin, Baie-Saint-Paul
117 Mrs. Atchée Tremblay, Baie-Saint-Paul
118 Mrs. Eugène Gravel, Baie-Saint-Paul
119 Mrs. Louis-Marie Simard, Baie-Saint-Paul
120 Mr. Émile Bouchard, Baie-Saint-Paul
121 Mr. Amédée Ménard, Baie-Saint-Paul
122 Mr. François Lavoie, Baie-Saint-Paul
124 Mr. Bertrand Lemieux, Baie-Saint-Paul
125 Mr. Joseph Mailloux, Cap-au-Corbeau
126 Mr. and Mrs. Alexis Zoël Tremblay, Les Éboulements
127 Mrs. Émerie Forgue, Pointe-au-Pic
132 Mrs. Grégoire Côté, L'Anse-Saint-Jean
133 Mr. and Mrs. Joseph Harvey, Notre-Dame-des-Monts
135 Mr. Élie Duchesne, Pointe-au-Pic
138 Mr. Lazare Bouchard, Les Éboulements
139 Mr. Joseph Dufour, Saint-Bernard-de-l'Île-aux-Coudres
141 Mr. Gérard Gagnon, La Baleine (Île aux Coudres)
142 Mrs. Élie Fortin, Baie-Saint-Paul
144 Mr. Joseph Bluteau, Petite-Rivière-Saint-François
145 Mr. Victor Simard, Petite-Rivière-Saint-François
146 Mr. and Mrs. Louis-Joseph Racine, Saint-Joachim (Montmorency)
147 Mr. Arthur Simard, Sainte-Anne-de-Beaupré
148 Mrs. Joseph Plante, Saint-Laurent (Île d'Orléans)
149 Mrs. Gédéon Coulombe, Saint-Laurent (Île d'Orléans)
151 Mr. Raoul Rouleau, Saint-Laurent (Île d'Orléans)
152 Mrs. Omer Langlois, Saint-Jean (Île d'Orléans)
153 Mrs. Jos Simard, Saint-Jean (Île d'Orléans)
156 Mrs. Léon Lepage, Saint-François (Île d'Orléans)
158 Mr. Létourneau, Sainte-Famille (Île d'Orléans)
159 Mrs. Yvonne Mercier, Château-Richer
160 Mrs. François Gauthier, Château-Richer
162 Mrs. Maurice Plante, Sainte-Pétronille (Île d'Orléans)
163 Mrs. Jean Plante, Saint-Henri

164 Mrs. Joseph Laprise, Saint-Jean-Chrysostome
165 Mr. Arcade Perreault, Scott-Jonction
166 Mr. Georges Drouin, Scott
167 Mr. Eugène Plante, Sainte-Famille (Île d'Orléans)
168 Mr. Hervé Giguère, Sainte-Marie-de-Beauce
169 Mr. Fortunat Gagné, Sainte-Marie-de-Beauce
170 Mr. Émile Landry, Sainte-Marie-de-Beauce
171 Mrs. Honoré Hébert, Sainte-Marie-de-Beauce
172 Mr. Alfred Turmel, Sainte-Marie-de-Beauce
173 Mrs. Eugène Giguère and Mrs. Valère Gilbert, Saint-Joseph-de-Beauce
174 Mr. Adrien Germain, Fortierville
175 Mr. Alfred Tousignant, Saint-Pierre-les-Becquets
176 Mrs. Jean-Paul Brisson, Fortierville
177 Mr. Adrien Germain, Fortierville
179 Mr. Égide Desrochers, Sainte-Croix-de-Lotbinière
180 Mr. Éléodore Drouin, Beaumont
182 Mrs. Alexandre Roy, Saint-Valier
183 Mr. Maurice Marquis, Montmagny
184 Mr. Maurice Leclerc, Saint-Jean-Port-Joli
185 *Idem*
186 Mr. Roméo Giasson, Saint-Jean-Port-Joli
187 Miss Marguerite Caron, Saint-Jean-Port-Joli
188 Mr. Albert Deschênes, Saint-Roch-des-Aulnaies
189 Mrs. Roland Létourneau, Saint-Roch-des-Aulnaies
190 Mrs. Hubert Létourneau, Saint-Roch-des-Aulnaies
192 Mr. Alphonse Dubé, Sainte-Anne-de-la-Pocatière
193 Mrs. Albert Dupont, Saint-Denis de-Kamouraska
194 Mrs. Gérard Lauzier, Kamouraska
195 Mr. Gérard Langlais, Kamouraska
196 Mr. Réal Dubé, Sainte-Hélène
197 Mr. Thomas Plourde, Saint-Pascal
198 Mr. Élisée Lévesque, Kamouraska
200 Mr. and Mrs. Laurent Bérubé, Trois-Pistoles
201 Mr. Hervé Bérubé, Trois-Pistoles
202 Mrs. Gonzague Bouchard, Sainte-Flavie
204 Mrs. Fernand Bélanger, Baie-des-Sables
205 Mrs. Thomas Boucher, Baie-des-Sables
206 Mrs. Joseph Fortin, Saint-Ulric
207 Mr. and Mrs. Georges Pelletier, Saint-Joachim-de-Tourelle
208 Mrs. Fernand Bernatché, Rivière-à-Claude
209 Mr. Aurel Bond, Petite Madeleine (Gaspé)
210 Mr. Louis-Marie Gaumond, Petite Madeleine (Gaspé)
211 Mrs. Edmond Gaumond, Petite Madeleine (Gaspé)
212 Mrs. Jean-Guy Caron, Grande-Vallée
213 Mrs. Adéoda Coulombe, Grande-Vallée
214 Mr. and Mrs. Alfred Lebreux, Petite-Vallée
215 Mrs. Jean-Baptiste Bédard, Champlain

Bibliography

Judicial Archives

Archives judiciaires de Montréal, greffes notariaux (Montreal Judicial Archives, notarial records)
Adhémar, Anthoine (1668–1714)
Adhémar, Jean-Baptiste (1714–54)
Basset, Bénigne (1657–99)
Archives judiciaires de Québec, greffes notariaux (Quebec City Judicial Archives, notarial records)
Audouart, Guillaume (1647–63)
Chambalon, Louis (1692–1716)
Duquet, Pierre (1663–87)
Fillion, Michel (1660–88)
Genaple, François (1682–1709)
Rageot, Gilles (1666–92)

Published and Unpublished Material

Alexandrin, Barbara, and Robert Bothwell
(1970). *Bibliography of the Material Culture of New France*. National Museum of Man, Publications in History, No. 4. Ottawa: National Museums of Canada. 32 pp.

Allaire, Uldéric S.
(1931). *Le chansonnier canadien.* Montreal: Beauchemin. 174 pp.

Anderson, Jay A.
(1970). "Scholarship on Contemporary American Folk Foodways". In *Ethnological Food Research in Europe and U.S.A.,* ed. by Nils-Arvid Bringeus and Gùntér Wiegelmann. Reports from the First International Symposium for Ethnological Food Research, Lund, Sweden, pp. 56–63.
(1976). "The Early Development of French-Canadian Foodways". In *The Folklore of Canada,* ed. by Edith Fowke. Toronto: McClelland & Stewart, pp. 91–99.

Barbeau, Marius
(1916a). *Contes populaires canadiens.* Journal of American Folklore 29(111): 1–136.
(1916b). *Le folklore canadien-français.* Ottawa: Royal Society of Canada. Proceedings and transactions, 1915, 3rd ser. 9(1): 449–81.
(1923). "La fournée au bon vieux temps". *In* Edmond-Joseph Massicotte, *Nos Canadiens d'autrefois.* Montreal: Granger. Unpaginated.
(1934). *Au coeur de Québec.* Montreal: Zodiaque. 200 pp.
(1937). *Québec où survit l'ancienne France.* Quebec: Garneau. 174 pp.
(1942). *Maîtres artisans de chez nous.* Montreal: Zodiaquè. 221 pp.

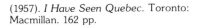

(1957). *I Have Seen Quebec*. Toronto: Macmillan. 162 pp.

Beaulieu, André, Jean Hamelin, and Benoît Bernier
(1969). *Guide d'histoire du Canada*. Quebec: Presses de l'université Laval. 540 pp.

Bélisle, Louis-Alexandre
(1957). *Dictionnaire général de la langue française au Canada*. Quebec: Bélisle.

Bergeron, René
(1947). *Dictionnaire humoristique*. 2nd ed. Montreal: Fides. 188 pp.

Berthelot, Hector
(1924). *Montréal, Le bon vieux temps*, Vol. 1. Montreal: Beauchemin. 124 pp.

Binford, Lewis R.
(1972). *An Archaeological Perspective*. New York: Seminar Press. 464 pp.

Binford, Sally R., and Lewis R. Binford, eds.
(1968). *New Perspectives in Archaeology*. Chicago: Aldine. 373 pp.

Boiteau, Georges
(1949). "Cahier manuscrit d'enquête (n° 3) pour le Musée national du Canada". Unpublished ms. Quebec: université Laval, Archives de Folklore. 50 pp.

Bouchard, Georges
(1917). *Premières semailles*. Quebec: Action sociale. 97 pp.
(1917-18). "Le vieux four de chez-nous". *Bulletin du parler français au Canada* 16: 406-11.
(1919). "Une culture nécessaire". *Terroir* 1(8): 48.
(1926). *Vieilles choses, vieilles gens*. Montreal: Beauchemin. 192 pp.

Clarke, David L.
(1968). *Analytical Archaeology*. London: Methuen. 684 pp.

Cloutier, J.-B.
(1888). *Recueil de leçons de choses*. Quebec: Darveau. 358 pp.

Dawson, Nora
(1960). *La vie traditionnelle à St-Pierre (Île d'Orléans)*. Archives de Folklore, Vol. 8. Quebec: Presses de l'université Laval. 190 pp.

Deetz, James
(1967). *Invitation to Archaeology*. Garden City, N.Y.: Published for the American Museum of Natural History by the Natural History Press. 150 pp.
(1968). "Late Man in North America: Archaeology of European Americans". In *Anthropological Archaeology in the Americas*. Washington, D.C.: The Anthropological Society of Washington, pp. 121-30.
(1969). "The Reality of the Pilgrim Fathers". *Natural History* 78(9): 32-45.
(1970). "Archaeology as a Social Science". *American Anthropological Association Bulletin* (special issue entitled *Current Directions in Anthropology*, ed. by Ann Fischer) 3(3, pt. 2): 115-25.
(1971). *Man's Imprint from the Past*. Boston: Little, Brown. 396 pp.
(1973). "Ceramics from Plymouth, 1635-1835: The Archaeological Evidence". In *Ceramics in America*, ed. by Ian M.G. Quimby. 18th Winterthur Conference, 1972. Charlotteville: University of Virginia Press, pp. 15-40.

Deetz, James, and Jay Anderson
(1972). "The Ethnogastronomy of Thanksgiving". *Saturday Review* 55(48): 29-39.

Diderot, D., and J.L. d'Alembert
(1782). *Encyclopédie ou Dictionnaire raisonné des sciences, des arts et des métiers*, Vol. 15. 2nd ed. Lausanne et Berne: Sociétés typographiques. (First ed., Paris: Briasson, 1751-65.)

Dionne, Narcisse-Eutrope
(1909). *Le parler populaire des Canadiens français, ou Lexique des canadianismes, des acadianismes, anglicismes, américanismes. . . .* Quebec: Laflamme & Proulx. 671 pp.

Dorais, Louis-Jacques
(1966). "La vie traditionnelle sur la côte de Beaupré". *Revue d'histoire de l'Amérique française* 19(4): 535-50.

Dorson, Richard M., ed.
(1972). *Folklore and Folklife: An Introduction*. Chicago: University of Chicago Press. 561 pp.

Dulong, Gaston
(1966). *Bibliographie linguistique du Canada français*. Quebec: Presses de l'université Laval. 166 pp.

Dupont, Jean-Claude
(1971). "Définitions des canadianismes folkloriques". Unpublished ms. Quebec: université Laval, Archives de Folklore.

Durand, Pierre, and Marcel Sarrau
(1973). *Le livre du pain*. Paris: Rocher.
114 pp.

**Falardeau, Jean-Charles,
Philippe Garigue, and Léon Gérin**
(1968). *Léon Gérin et l'habitant de
Saint-Justin*. Montreal: Presses de
l'Université de Montréal. 179 pp.

Fauteux, Joseph-Noël
(1927). *Essai sur l'industrie au Canada
sous le régime français*. 2 vols. Quebec:
Proulx, Imprimeur du Roi. 572 pp.

Fernandez, James W.
(1972). "Persuasions and Performances:
Of the Beast in Every Body . . . and the
Metaphors of Everyman". *Daedalus*
101(1): 39–60.

Gagnon, Ernest
(1908). *Chansons populaires au
Canada*. 7th ed. Montreal: Beauchemin.
350 pp.

**Galarneau, Claude, and Elzéar
Lavoie, eds.**
(1966). *France et Canada français du
XVIe au XXe siècle*. Cahiers de l'Institut
d'Histoire, No. 7. Quebec: Presses de
l'université Laval. 322 pp.

Girard, Charles
(1967). "Le vieux four". *La Voix du lac
Saint-Jean,* Saint-Félicien, 12 Oct.,
p. 17.

Glassie, Henry H.
(1968). *Pattern in the Material Folk
Culture of the Eastern United States*.
University of Pennsylvania Monographs
in Folklore and Folklife, No. 1. Philadel-
phia: University of Pennsylvania Press.
376 pp.

Hamelin, Jean
(1960). *Économie et Société en Nouvelle-
France*. Cahier de l'Institut d'Histoire,
No. 3. Quebec: Presses de l'université
Laval. 137 pp.

Harris, Richard Colebrook
(1966). *The Seigneurial System in Early
Canada: A Geographical Study*.
Madison: University of Wisconsin Press;
Quebec: Presses de l'université Laval.
247 pp.

Heagle, Walter D.
(1968). "Baking Industry". *Encyclopedia
Canadiana*, pp. 284–85.

Hémon, Louis
(1957). *Maria Chapdelaine*. Montreal:
Fides. 189 pp. (Available in English
under the same title. Transl. by W.H.
Blake. New York: Macmillan, 1921.
288 pp.)

Kalm, Pehr
(1966). *The America of 1750: Peter
Kalm's Travels in North America,* ed.
by Adolph B. Benson. 2 vols. New
York: Dover. 797 pp.

Kniffen, Fred
(1960). "The Outdoor Oven in
Louisiana". *Louisiana History* 1(1):
25–35.

Laberge, Albert
(1918). *La Scouine*. Montreal: Édition
privée, Imprimerie modèle, Réédition-
Québec. 134 pp.

Labignette, Jean-Éric
(1964). "La farine dans la Nouvelle-
France". *Revue d'histoire de l'Amérique
française* 17(4): 490–503.

Labrie, Arthur
(1970). *Le moulin de Beaumont*.
Quebec: Arthur Labrie. 52 pp.

Lacourcière, Luc
(1950). "Notes linguistiques sur le
dernier-né". Université Laval, *Archives
de Folklore*, Vol. 4. Montreal: Fides,
p. 76.
(1966). "La tradition orale au Canada".
In *France et Canada français du XVIe
au XXe siècle,* ed. by Claude Galarneau
and Elzéar Lavoie. Cahiers de l'Institut
d'Histoire, No. 7. Quebec: Presses de
l'université Laval, pp. 223–31.

Larouche, Jean-Claude
(1971). *Alexis le Trotteur*. Montreal:
Éditions du Jour. 297 pp.

Lavoie, Thomas
(1971). "Les métaphores zoomorphiques
dans le parler québécois (Le Saguenay)". *Protée* 1(3): 51–60.
(1972). *Enquêtes sur les parlers français
de Charlevoix, du Saguenay, du lac St-
Jean et de la Côte-Nord*. Chicoutimi:
Université du Québec à Chicoutimi.
225 pp.

**Leach, MacEdward, and Henry
Glassie**
(1968). *A Guide for Collectors of Oral
Traditions and Folk Cultural Material in
Pennsylvania*. Harrisburg: Pennsylvania

Historical and Museum Commission. 70 pp.

Lefebvre, Fernand
(1961). "La fabrication du pain au Canada". *Bulletin des Recherches historiques* 67(3): 99–104.

Lemieux, Germain
(1965). "La chanson folklorique canadienne-française". In *La chanson française*. Montreal: Bellarmin, pp. 49–62.

Lévi-Strauss, Claude
(1958). *Anthropologie structurale.* Paris: Plon. 452 pp.
(1962). *La pensée sauvage.* Paris: Plon. 380 pp.

Liger, Louis, Sieur d'Auxerre
(1732). *La nouvelle maison rustique.* 4th ed. 2 vols. Paris: Prudhomme. 1,942 pp.

Long, Amos, Jr.
(1963). "Outdoor Bakeovens in Berks". *Historical Review of Berks County* 28(1): 11–14, 16–29.
(1964). "Bakeovens in the Pennsylvania Folk-Culture". *Pennsylvania Folklife* 14(2): 16–29.
(1965). "Pennsylvania Summer-Houses and Summer-Kitchens". *Pennsylvania Folklife* 15(1): 10–19.

Maltais, Jean-Eudes, Madeleine Maltais, and Raoul Lapointe
(1970). *Collection Villeneuve.* Chicoutimi: Université du Québec à Chicoutimi. 428 pp.

Marie-Ursule, c.s.j., Soeur
(1951). *"Civilisation traditionnelle des Lavallois".* Archives de Folklore, Vol. 5–6. Quebec: Presses de l'université Laval. 403 pp.

Massicotte, Édouard-Zotique
(1924). "La vie dans les chantiers". *Almanach du Peuple.* Montreal: Beauchemin, pp. 311–20.
(1926). *Procession de la Saint-Jean-Baptiste en 1924–25.* Montreal: Beauchemin. 315 pp.
(1932). "La récolte du diable". *Bulletin des Recherches historiques* 38(11): 668–72.
(1934). "Le diable bafoué". *Bulletin des Recherches historiques* 40(5): 304–06.
(1941). "La boulangerie à Montréal avant 1760". *Bulletin des Recherches historiques* 47(3): 79–84.

Mead, Margaret
(1964). *Food Habit Research: Problems of the 1960's.* Washington, D.C.: National Academy of Sciences and National Research Council. 39 pp.

Mook, Maurice A.
(1971). "Bread Baking in Mifflin County, Pennsylvania: Commentary for the Documentary Film in the 'Encyclopedia Cinematographica' ". *Pennsylvania Folklife* 21(1): 42–45.

Morisset, Gérard
(1949). *L'architecture en Nouvelle-France.* Quebec: Collections Champlain. 150 pp.
(1958). "Quebec: The Country House". *Canadian Geographical Journal* 57(6): 178–95.

Nadeau, Aurel
(1916). *La grande erreur du pain blanc.* Bulletin, No. 24. Quebec: Ministère de l'Agriculture. 85 pp.

Pahin, Mani Han, and Marie-Jeanne Basile
(1973). *Innuapminwan/Ethnocuisine montagnaise.* Nordicana, No. 35. Quebec: université Laval, Centre d'Études nordiques. 43 pp.

Paré, Eugénie
(1934, 1940). *Le pain de ménage.* Bulletin, No. 131. Quebec: Ministère de l'Agriculture. 1st ed., 1934, 32 pp.; 2nd ed., 1940, 30 pp.

Pouinard, Alfred-Antonin
(1950). "Recherches sur la musique d'origine française en Amérique du Nord: Canada et Louisiane". Ph.D. dissertation, université Laval.

Quebec (Province)
(1927). *Vieux manoirs, vieilles maisons.* Quebec: Imprimeur du Roi. 376 pp.

Rosaldo, Michel Zimbalist
(1972). "Metaphors and Folk Classification". *Southwestern Journal of Anthropology* 28(1): 83–99.

Rousseau, Jacques
(1938). "L'histoire du pain". *Le Devoir,* 23 July, p. 12.
(1942). "La civilisation du blé". *Le Devoir,* 23 May, p. 12.

Rousseau, Jacques, and Madeleine Rousseau
(1950). "Charmes et merveilleux". Université Laval, *Archives de Folklore*, Vol. 4. Montreal: Fides, pp. 77–85.

Roy, Carmen
(1962). *La littérature orale en Gaspésie*. 2nd ed. National Museum of Canada, Bulletin 134. 389 pp.

Roy, Pierre-Georges
(1923). "Proverbes à propos de noces". *Bulletin des Recherches historiques* 29(10): 310.
(1924). "Le four banal dans la Nouvelle-France". *Bulletin des Recherches historiques* 30(9): 257–60.
(1928). *L'Île d'Orléans*. Quebec: Proulx, Imprimerie du Roi. 505 pp.
(1931). "Le four banal dans la Nouvelle-France". *Les petites choses de notre histoire*, ser. 6, ed. by Pierre-Georges Roy. Lévis, Quebec: Quotidien, pp. 144–49.
(1944). "Les jeteux de sorts". *Les petites choses de notre histoire,* ser. 7, ed. by Pierre-Georges Roy. Quebec: Garneau, pp. 77–79.

Roy, Pierre-Georges, ed.
(1895–1924). *Bulletin des Recherches historiques,* Vols. 1–30. Lévis, Quebec: Société des Études historiques.

Roy, Pierre-Georges, and Antoine Roy
(1942–56). *Inventaire des greffes de notaire du régime français*. Vols. 1–18. Quebec: Archives de la Province.

Russell, Willis
(1857). *Quebec: As It Was and As It Is*. Quebec: P. Lamoureux. 160 pp.

Savard, Félix-Antoine
(1943). *L'Abatis*. Montreal: Fides. 209 pp.

Séguin, Robert-Lionel
(1967). *Civilisation traditionnelle de l'habitant aux XVIIᵉ et XVIIIᵉ siècles*. Montreal: Fides. 701 pp.
(1968). *La maison en Nouvelle-France*. National Museum of Canada, Bulletin 226. 107 pp.
(1969). "Quelques techniques et métiers traditionnels d'antan". *Cahier des Dix* 34: 165–80.
(1972). *Les ustensiles en Nouvelle-France*. Montreal: Leméac. 143 pp.

Société du Parler français au Canada
(1930). *Glossaire du parler français au Canada*. Quebec: Action sociale. 709 pp.

Société Saint-Jean-Baptiste de Montréal
(1917). *La Corvée*. Deuxième concours littéraire de la société. Montreal: Société Saint-Jean-Baptiste. 239 pp.

Steward, Julian Haynes
(1955). *Theory of Culture Change*. Urbana: University of Illinois Press. 244 pp.

Tremblay, Victor
(1968). *Histoire du Saguenay*. Publication de la Société Historique du Saguenay, No. 21. Chicoutimi, Quebec: Librairie Régionale. 465 pp.

Trudel, Marcel
(1968). *Initiation à la Nouvelle-France*. Montreal: Holt, Rinehart and Winston. 323 pp.

Vachon, André
(1962). *Histoire du notariat canadien, 1621–1960*. Quebec: Presses de l'université Laval. 209 pp.

Valin, Roch
(1947). "Alexis Centaure". *L'Enseignement secondaire au Canada* 26(8): 312–18.